MISSED CHANCES

A Rob Mathews Sports Season
Book 6

Mac McGowan

CV-LW Books

Copyright © 2023 by Terry McGowan

All rights reserved.

No part of this publication may be reproduced, distributed, or transmitted in any form or by any means, including photocopying, recording, or other electronic or mechanical methods, without the prior written permission of the publisher, except as permitted by U.S. copyright law. For permission requests, please contact Terry McGowan at mac.mcgowan23@gmail.com

The story, all names, characters, and incidents portrayed in this production are fictitious. No identification with actual persons (living or deceased), places, buildings, and products is intended or should be inferred.

Book Cover by 100 Covers

Published by CV-LW Books 1st edition 2023

ISBN# 978-1-962126-21-2   Paperback version

DEDICATION

The Rob Mathews Sports Series is dedicated first to three of our 13 grandchildren. Our oldest, JT, began reading the series as a ten-year-old. He was patient, as there were only two completed books when he started, and so he read the first few books several times. His enthusiasm pushed me to continue writing. Dean and Gavin were next, beginning to read them when they were 12 and ten. They started the series as I was working on Book 11, and again, their enthusiasm and enjoyment of the books drove me to the finish line. The series is also dedicated to my wonderful wife, Suzy, who put up with my countless hours on the computer, writing, editing, editing, and editing! Her positive comments after helping edit the first three books also pushed me to finish. Many thanks to you all!

Preface

A few words about this book and the Rob Mathews Sports Series. While each book could certainly be read "on its own," I think readers will find the series a much more enjoyable experience if starting with Book One (Fresh Start) and reading them in order until completion. This series was written in many ways as one long, gigantic book. Plot lines are established in Book One (Fresh Start) that run through the entire series, and several main characters are added as the series progresses, most notably in Book Four (Last Chance), Book Eight (New Normal), and Book Nine (Best Case). Reading the books out of order might cause you to scratch your head about who a character is or why they are doing this or that.

In addition, many character traits and attitudes are established early and subtly change as young kids mature into young adults. Since the series travels from the beginning of 9th grade to the end of 12th grade, some behavior needs to mature slowly over time as it would in the real world. Some issues simply would not change over the course of three months, the rough time span of each book. For instance, the main character's and his male friend's obsession with appearance gradually changes, showing positive improvement as early as Book Two (Game Plan) and Book Three (Team Players), and fully changes by Book Six (Missed Chances). However, please note that both teenage boys and girls do, in real life, have and express opinions about the appearance of the opposite sex.

Finally, should some of the sports action described be hard to believe, I assure you I have personally experienced or seen everything described actually happen!

Enjoy the series, and thank you for reading!

CHAPTER 1
MARCH-SOPHOMORE YEAR

THE sun quickly faded as the late afternoon sky went from gray to black. All 18 Hillsdale High School Varsity Baseball players sat shivering in their first base dugout listening to Coach Dave Wilson.

Coach Wilson was covered up against the cold, masking his California Surfer good looks and the chiseled body of the former defensive back at the University of Southern California.

"Tomorrow will be game one . . ." Coach Wilson pronounced. "You basketball players will sit . . . these guys who have been out here for a while deserve to play tomorrow."

Coach Wilson's eyes passed over Rob Mathews, Bill "Trip" McHenry, Brad Wallace, and Josh Lee, who all had played in last Saturday's heartbreaking loss to Valley Christian in the Basketball Sectional Finals.

"I think next year," Coach Wilson said with a smile, "I need to think about pushing back the date of our first game . . . if you guys get past Sectionals next year, there is no telling when we might get you out here."

The team laughed together . . . but they knew that Coach Wilson meant what he said. With Trip McHenry staying at Hillsdale, the sky was the limit for the basketball team . . . and probably for the football and baseball teams as well.

"Get a good night's sleep . . . and come out ready to play hard," Coach Wilson concluded his talk. "We'll see you tomorrow at 3:00 pm."

With that, most of the players jumped up, hurriedly got their gear together, and headed home to get warm.

Rob Mathews sat alone at first, pulling his jacket tight around his neck for warmth. His short brown hair was tucked neatly under his cap, and his strong, toned body weighed about 200 pounds and stretched nearly six-foot-two inches long. He sat just relaxing for a moment . . . with the hint of a smile playing around his mouth. He let out a long, contented sigh. *I love baseball,* Rob thought as he gazed onto the field as the sun disappeared and darkness took over. *There is just so much more time to enjoy the moment.*

The last flicker of light barely illuminated the Hillsdale Baseball/Softball Complex that Hillsdale High and the Hillsdale youth leagues called home. Lights from the parking lot flickered on, allowing Rob to take in the four fields and the snack bar/team rooms/restrooms buildings that Coach Dave Wilson had managed to get built since he came to Hillsdale two years ago. *I sure love sitting here . . . in this dugout . . .* Rob daydreamed. *It feels like home!*

Rob felt a presence and looked up to see Bill "Trip" McHenry towering over him. Trip, six-foot-six inches and 235 pounds of muscled bulk, had his gear in his hands, ready to roll.

Trip snatched his Hillsdale High baseball hat from his head, ran his fingers through his dark brown, wavy hair, and smiled the smile the girls at Hillsdale High loved to see.

"Ready to go?" Trip asked Rob, nodding in the direction of Buck Buckman, who was waiting to walk home with the pair.

"Nah, I'm just going to sit a minute," Rob answered.

Trip lowered himself onto the bench next to Rob and motioned Buck to sit as well.

The tall, slender but strong, lightning-fast center-fielder for the Pirates nodded, glided to the bench, and sat next to Trip. *Man, Buck moves like a young Willie Mays,* Rob thought, watching his friend plop down. *To think his great-grandfather played with Mays in the old Negro Leagues back in the 1940s. Amazing!*

"Does it feel like we just got off a wild ride at the County Fair?" Rob asked Trip with a long sigh.

Trip mulled this over and finally replied, "You know, you're right . . . that's exactly how it feels. Just sittin' here . . . it feels good to just sit for a minute."

"I know what you mean," Buck interjected. "I felt that way after the "Pick" game. Suddenly, football was over, and I could just relax . . . but you guys had to step it up right away with Varsity basketball . . . I just had JV basketball and then some time off before baseball started. You guys better enjoy the next few days . . . your first game will be Friday."

"Yeah," Rob said dreamily. "It's been a wild year so far. I sure hope we end this season by winning our last game . . . and that last game is the Sectional Finals."

"Amen to that!" Buck exclaimed.

"That would be nice," Trip McHenry added.

"What do you say we make that happen!" Buck exclaimed with a laugh.

"Yeah . . . I could go for that! I'm getting tired of being a loser in the last game of the season," Rob said with a heavy sigh. "Real tired . . ."

CHAPTER 2
MARCH-SOPHOMORE YEAR

*T*HE trio sat silently for a couple of minutes, enjoying the quiet.

"Next year, you'll be in the same position we are, Buck," Rob finally said. "You know, going from basketball playoffs right into baseball."

"Ah, I don't think so, man," Buck replied slowly.

Rob jerked his head toward Buck, leaning forward to see around Trip's massive frame.

"What? What do you mean?" Rob asked in surprise.

"I think I've played my last high school basketball game," Buck said with a short laugh. "You guys are too good for me . . . I can't play at that level. Besides, I think it's time for me to focus more on baseball in the winter . . . there is no way I'm playing basketball in college . . . but baseball, that's my ticket to school."

"You still going to play football?" Trip asked in concern. "We need you to win back the "Pick!"

The "Pick," a gold-plated Miners Pick awarded to the winner of the Hillsdale High-Pine Bluff High football game each fall, was always at the top of everybody's mind . . . if they cared about Hillsdale High School sports, that is. The series, separated by just one slim game after nearly 100 years, would end in two years when Pine Bluff merged with Cashtown, making them too large for Hillsdale to play in football anymore. Hillsdale had to go two-for-two the next two years to keep the "Pick" forever . . . the biggest goal in all of Hillsdale!

"Yeah, I won't miss bringing back the "Pick!" Buck answered. "But basketball . . . it's fun . . . I like playing . . . but I don't like to sit . . . I'd spend most of basketball season riding the bench . . . and baseball is number one. I'll spend a lot of the winter on conditioning and hitting. Next year is the big recruitment year for me."

"Where do you want to go?" Trip asked.

"I'm thinking maybe Oregon State . . . Arizona or Arizona State . . . maybe USC, UCLA or Cal . . . I think I have a chance to play at a powerhouse," Buck said tentatively, not wanting to sound cocky.

"No doubt about it," Rob said earnestly. "You got the talent."

Trip shook his head in agreement.

"Agreed," Trip said quickly. "Choose USC or UCLA . . . that way, we'd both be in L.A."

"You're stuck on USC, huh?" Buck laughed.

"Yeah . . . I'll look at all offers," Trip answered with a cocky grin. "But I'm going to Southern Cal . . . it's in my blood."

"What about you, Rob?" Buck asked. "Started to think about it yet?"

"Not really," Rob answered sincerely. "I'm still not sure what sport I want to play in college . . . I'll start thinking about it after this baseball season. Going to have to pick just one sport in college . . . unless I go to a small D2 or D3 school . . . I could maybe do two sports at a small school."

"Oh, come on, "Wonder Boy!" Trip said incredulously. "You're too good to go to a small school . . . those D1 schools are going to be offering you a ride . . . come play basketball with me at USC."

"Sorry, man . . . he's playing baseball with me . . . wherever I end up," Buck said with a burst of laughter.

The trio laughed hard and sat back, reflecting.

Finally, Rob stood up and gathered his gear together.

"You guys ready yet?" he asked with mock irritation. "I've been waiting on you guys for hours!"

Laughter filled the dugout again.

The threesome went out into the darkening night, thankful for the illumination from the street lights, and made their way home, laughing and joking all the way.

Rob was the first to break off as he turned down his street, while Buck and Trip headed around the corner to their homes.

Suddenly alone, walking toward his house, Rob realized he was getting older. *Geez,* he thought, *I really need to start thinking about college. Where do I want to go? Big school? Small school? Big city? Small town?*

He slowed his pace as he neared his house and stopped to gaze into a fully lit window on the second story of the house next door to his own.

He saw Allison Pierce standing at the window and gazing back at him. Her long, straight, black hair hung nearly to her waist, and her oversized glasses dominated her face. *Except when she smiles,* Rob thought. *And, then, her eyes dominate . . . that's if the glare from her mouth full of braces doesn't blind you! She's so geeky looking . . . but so special, too!*

Rob waved a hand in greeting, and Allison smiled and waved back.

Good ol' goofy, Allison, Rob pondered. *What would I do without her? Guess I don't have to worry about that now.*

Rob waved again, turned, and hurried into his house to see his Mom.

***

*A*s he walked by Allison's, he saw his house was lit up. The inviting front porch was bathed by the porch lights and came complete with rocking chairs and a porch swing. The two-story "A" frame home had many large windows now throwing light onto the walkway ... and let in tons of natural light during the day.

Rob bounded up the steps and into the house and was immediately toasty warm ... both body and soul. Not only was the heat turned up nicely ... but his Mom, Emily Mathews, smiled at him in greeting, and Rob knew he was truly home.

Rob smiled, waved, and looked past her into the brightly lit kitchen/great room and dining room/solarium. He smiled again, thinking of all the good times they'd had in those rooms since they moved in almost two years ago.

Some bad times, too, Rob reflected. *Dad died almost two years ago. I miss him so much. I wonder ... I wonder ... I sure wish he was here to enjoy this, too.*

Rob shook himself, turned, walked back to the entry, and climbed the stairs toward his bedroom. Once upstairs, he walked along the landing ... looking down into his living room below. *Yeah ... even with the bad ... this is really home. I love it here!*

CHAPTER 3
MARCH-SOPHOMORE YEAR

*A*LL through the game the next day, Rob Mathews felt off. He wasn't used to sitting when he was healthy . . . and here he was, sitting and watching his Hillsdale Pirates play their first game of the season without him.

It's just weird, Rob thought.

He gazed over at his friend Trip McHenry and knew he was feeling similar thoughts. *It's just one game,* Rob reminded himself. *Friday, we play!*

Rob decided to sit back and enjoy it. The weather had warmed up a bit from yesterday . . . but not much. The guys on the bench huddled together and occasionally stomped their feet to keep warm.

Between innings, those not playing, including Rob, would get up and stretch, walk out of the dugout to look into the stands, and wave at friends or family . . . or to just be seen!

Fortunately, Hillsdale's first game was against a perennially weak team, and the Pirates were handling them with ease. Having jolted out to a 4-0 lead after one, they stretched it to 8-1 after five innings. Buck Buckman was leading the way with three hits, four stolen bases, and three runs . . . and a great catch in center field that nobody in the park except Buck could have caught!

After the bottom of the 6th, Rob sauntered out of the dugout and scanned the sparse crowd. With the cold, and the game in hand, most of the fans had departed . . . but hanging in there were the Three Amigos . . . Rob's Mom, Emily, his Grandpa Russell, and, of course, next-door neighbor, Allison Pierce!

The trio sat huddled together, fighting off the icy wind as best they could, and all three smiled and waved as they caught Rob's eye.

What are they doing here? Rob wondered. *I told them I wouldn't be playing today. Oh, well . . . I guess they are the definition of die-hard fans.*

Rob took a long look at his Mom and smiled warmly at her. Just under 40, Emily was bundled up, but her youthful good looks still shone through. Her longish, auburn-brown hair was piled inside a winter cap, but her girl-next-door, fresh-faced beauty, beamed back at him and made him feel good.

As he watched, the three of them stood up and moved around to try and warm up. Rob noticed that Emily, about five-foot-six, was now the shortest of the group. *Allison looks like she has passed Mom up,* Rob realized.

Grandpa Russell still cut a fine figure at six-foot-two and just under 200 pounds. His gray hair peeked out from under a Hillsdale High baseball cap . . . but he still looked like the athlete he was as a kid. Grandma Russell, who looked like the proverbial Mrs. Santa Claus, had stayed home . . . too cold. *She still is the smart one,* Rob chuckled.

The trio sat down as Rob headed back to the dugout for the top of the 7th and hopefully the last inning. Rob noticed Allison was in the middle . . . *so she could talk to both Mom and Grandpa . . . Mom for the girl's take of the game . . . Grandpa for the technical part. Allison really is becoming a sports fan,* Rob marveled as he turned to sit back down. *If she just wasn't so goofy-looking.*

POP. A short pause. POP.

The two loud POPS caught Rob's attention, and he looked to find the source.

Rob smiled and shook his head with a smile. The POP came from the ball hitting catcher Toby Tyler's glove . . . a resounding noise caused by the force of an Ethan "Hulk" Thomas fastball hitting leather.

"Man, he throws hard," Trip McHenry said. "Got to be in the mid-90s!"

"At least," Rob answered as he stared at the freshman pitcher.

Hulk Thomas stood six-foot-four . . . but looked taller . . . because he weighed 250 pounds! It wasn't all fat . . . and it wasn't all muscle. Hulk was a giant kid who still had some baby fat . . . and if he lost that . . . and worked out a little, he would be downright scary. *He reminds me of Edgar Garcia,* Rob remembered. *Edgar sure transformed freshman year!*

"Does this guy play football?" Trip asked.

"He played Freshman for the first half . . . then came up with Toby Tyler about the time you showed up. Weren't you paying attention?" Rob answered.

"Not really . . ." Trip admitted sheepishly. "Didn't expect to need to pay attention . . . thought I'd be long gone before next football season!"

"He's slimmed down since football," Rob said in surprise.

Trip looked back at him quizzically. "Was he bigger than this?"

"He was huge," Rob laughed. "I think Coach Wilson has been working with him on losing some weight and turning it into muscle . . . he's hoping he can help anchor the offensive and defensive lines next year."

"By himself," Trip laughed, and Rob joined in.

"Nice kid," Rob continued. "Shy . . . competitive . . . doesn't like to lose or not do well."

"I like the sound of that," Trip mused as he watched Hulk's last warmup pitch sail high over Toby Tyler's head and to the backstop.

"Jussssst a little bit high," Trip quipped.

Coach Wilson walked up to the pair and leaned close to Rob.

"Hulk's going to be your project this year . . . if you're up for it," Coach Wilson said quietly to Rob. "He throws so darn hard . . . but he's not always sure where it's going. If he lays off a little to get it in the strike zone . . . the good hitters will rip him."

Rob nodded and suddenly became more serious . . . gazing intently at Hulk Thomas.

"We need to tweak his motion . . . get his release point more consistent," Coach Wilson said. "And, you need to teach him . . . probably a cutter first . . . then a change . . . he needs more movement with the hard stuff . . . and we have to get him mixing his speeds."

Rob nodded at Coach Wilson and watched Hulk Thomas peer in for his first sign.

Toby Tyler flashed for the fastball, and Hulk reared back and threw the ball as hard as he could . . . and the ball sailed three feet over Toby's head to the backstop again.

The next pitch was lower . . . maybe only a foot over Toby's outstretched glove as he jumped for the pitch . . . but it was directly over the batter's head . . . and the batter suddenly wanted no part of standing in against Hulk Thomas.

Toby trotted to the mound, said a few words, and got back behind the plate.

Strike one . . . right down the middle. Strike two, right down the middle. The next pitch sailed to the backstop.

The last pitch was straight down the middle, and the batter swung and missed . . . stepping so far in the bucket that his bat could have never reached the heart of the plate.

And, so it went. After three walks and two more strikeouts, Hulk Thomas completed the 8-1 victory and strode heavily off the field with a satisfied grin.

Coach Wilson stopped Rob and quickly pulled him close.

"See what I mean?" Coach Wilson asked. "Think you can help?"

"I think so," Rob said hopefully. "My house . . . after practice "practices" for him could do the trick . . . just like Kenny Johnson last year."

"That's just what I was thinking," Coach Wilson said with a smile. "Thanks, Rob!"

CHAPTER 4
MARCH–SOPHOMORE YEAR

*F**RIDAY* could not arrive fast enough for Rob Mathews. He was anxious to get some game time and had worked hard to prove to Coach Wilson . . . and more importantly to his teammates . . . that he deserved to be on the field.

Trip McHenry felt the same way . . . but he felt the pressure just a little bit more. *They know I can play basketball,* Trip thought, *but that's my game. Baseball . . . not so much. I've got to produce!*

Both boys had done plenty on Wednesday and Thursday to convince Coach Wilson they deserved to be in the starting lineup on Friday. They had hustled, shown outstanding leadership, great attitudes, and . . . most importantly . . . great talent during all of the drills and simulated game situations that Coach Wilson had thrown at them.

Come Friday, Rob was penciled in as the starting shortstop, hitting number-three, and Trip was hitting right behind him in the cleanup spot and playing first base.

Brad Wallace was getting the nod on the hill, and Josh Lee completed the Varsity Basketball players who were in the starting lineup . . . Josh was playing third and hitting in the eight-spot.

Mark Porter, senior second baseman, was hitting second for the Pirates, while senior Bruce Smithers caught and batted fifth. Smithers, who suffered a crushing leg injury last season, causing him to miss both football and basketball seasons this year, was hoping his swan song at Hillsdale would be successful.

His leg injury was healed enough to do some catching, but the year-long grind might be too much, so Coach Wilson was planning to give Toby Tyler time behind the plate as well. But today, Tyler was the Designated Hitter in the sixth slot.

Rounding out the lineup were the outfielders. Buck Buckman led off . . . and led the Pirate's offense with a high on-base percentage that translated into leading the league in runs scored last year . . . as a freshman!

Two juniors were playing the corners. Matt Bryant, tall and rangy, patrolled left field and batted seventh, while Gavin Ford roamed right field and used his speed and keen eye to become somewhat of a second leadoff hitter in the nine-spot. He figured to score a lot of runs this year ahead of the big guns at the top of the order.

While Coach Wilson had scheduled a soft beginning on Tuesday, Friday's opponent was the much larger and much stronger team from the Sacramento area . . . Braxton High . . . the team that had beaten Hillsdale 61-60 in a memorable game at the beginning of the basketball season.

Braxton had been impressed enough with the basketball program to seek out a game with the Pirates . . . and make the trek up into the foothills to play in Hillsdale.

Being a preseason game . . . and just game two of the preseason . . . Coach Dave Wilson's plan was to see as many of his probable pitchers as possible against a strong team. His plan had Brad Wallace going the first two innings, followed by junior left-hander Jose Rivera, Josh Lee, Trip McHenry, Rob Mathews, and Hulk Thomas each for one inning.

Coach Wilson also hoped to get everyone on the squad at least one at bat . . . but he also wanted to make a good showing against Braxton . . . and several guys who were being replaced in the starting lineup by the basketball players had all played the entire game in the opener on Tuesday . . . so may not see action today.

Brad Wallace opened up the game with a strike and then dazzled Braxton with his assortment of cutters, curves, and changeups for a 1-2-3 first inning.

On came the Hillsdale offense, and Buck Buckman got things started . . . as usual . . . with a sharp single to right-center. Mark Porter laid down a sacrifice bunt, and up came Rob Mathews with Buck in scoring position.

"Here we go . . . !" Grandpa Russell crowed in the Hillsdale bleachers.

He was surrounded by Emily and Allison, and Grandma Russell . . . the weather had warmed up sufficiently for her to be there . . . and they all smiled at Grandpa Russell's constant belief in Rob.

He wasn't wrong.

Rob wasted no time and slashed the first pitch on a line toward shortstop. Buck hesitated at second to see if the screaming liner would make it over the shortstop's glove . . . it did by a good two inches . . . and it sailed out to left field.

Buck dashed toward third and rounded the corner expecting to make for the plate, but Coach Wilson put on the brakes and held him at third base.

Buck looked up questionably at Coach Wilson as time was called after the ball was returned to the pitcher.

"He hit it too hard," Coach Wilson laughed, nodding over at Rob. "Left-fielder had it coming back in just as you rounded the bag."

"Right," Buck laughed. "And, don't make an out going to third or home with less than two outs . . . correct."

"Correct," Coach Wilson laughed.

Now it was the first big moment of the game . . . and the season for Trip McHenry. *First and third . . . one out . . . we just need to pick up a run here . . . get a lead,* Trip thought. *Don't try to do too much.*

Trip looked for Coach Wilson's signs, settled in, and took a strike. The next pitch sailed high and outside. Trip looked to Coach Wilson, half expecting to see Rob get the steal sign at first.

No, no, Trip realized. *The first baseman is holding Rob close at first . . . there's a huge hole between first and second . . . a ground ball to that side gets us a run . . . don't get greedy . . . ground ball to the right side or a sac fly . . . just hit it solid.*

Hit it solid is what Trip did . . . but he hit it too close to the second baseman.

The ball clanged loudly off Trip's aluminum bat and rocketed to the left of the second baseman on its way to right field and a 1-0 Hillsdale lead . . . but the second sacker moved quickly to his left and speared the shot on the second hop. He wheeled and fired to the shortstop, covering the bag at second for the force out on a sliding Rob Mathews.

The shortstop avoided contact with Rob, planted . . . and fired a strike to first to complete the double play and take the wind out of Trip, the Hillsdale Pirates, Grandpa Russell, and the rest of the Hillsdale crowd.

Hope that's not a sign of things to come, Grandpa Russell mused as he sat down heavily. *Can't afford to miss chances!*

CHAPTER 5
MARCH–SOPHOMORE YEAR

*T*HE pitchers definitely seemed to be ahead of the hitters in this one, as is often the case early in the season.

Brad Wallace breezed through the second inning, and Jose Rivera, making his second Varsity appearance, made quick work of Braxton in the third . . . the Hillsdale pitchers had a perfect game through three innings, and Coach Wilson was delighted with his pitching against such a strong team.

However, the Pirates could not generate any offense either. Six up and six down over the next two innings kept the game scoreless going into the top of the fourth.

Josh Lee came on to make his Varsity pitching debut, and the righthander quickly got the first two outs on a pop-up to short and a grounder to third. The freshman, a budding three-sport star, was smooth as silk on the hill and exuded a quiet confidence wherever he played.

But . . . his first pitch to the next hitter, Braxton's powerful number three-hitter . . . was a mistake . . . to put it mildly. Josh hung a curve ball, trying to sneak strike one, and it sat there as if it were on a tee . . . and the Braxton slugger demolished the pitch and deposited it far over the left-center field fence . . . and Braxton was on top 1-0.

Josh got the next hitter to bounce out and got the Pirates into the dugout to hit. Rob and Trip singled with one out, bringing Bruce Smithers to the plate with runners at the corners, with a chance to do some damage.

The crowd perked up again . . . with Grandpa Russell leading the charge.

"This is it!" Grandpa Russell screamed out. "Come on, Pirates . . . pick this runner up!"

The rest of the crowd joined in. Donnie Fields and Christina Craft . . . sitting just below Grandpa Russell, started to chant, "PIRATES . . . PIRATES . . .!"

Allison Pierce and Emily joined in, and Allison looked around to see Stephanie Miller and Phil Boyer sitting together with a mob of kids, and they all joined in the chant.

Bruce Smithers, the team leader in RBI's last year until his injury, confidently strode to the plate and smiled at the chant.

He worked the count to two balls and two strikes and then ripped a shot . . . right at the third baseman . . . who never had to move . . . until he caught the ball and dove headlong toward the third base bag, trying to double Rob off.

Rob also dove toward the bag and beat the diving third baseman by an eyelash. Two outs. Runners at the corners. Toby Tyler striding to the plate.

Toby could always hit. He was the RBI leader of the JV squad last year . . . and would probably settle into the fifth spot after Bruce Smithers graduated. He knew he could hit . . . and knew he could drive in runs.

The first pitch to Toby was a nothing-fastball right down the gut . . . Toby didn't miss it. He hit a screaming line drive straight up the middle, and the crowd gasped . . . and then groaned as the pitcher somehow threw up his glove in self-defense and snagged the searing line drive. Inning over.

***

*T*RIP McHenry took the mound to start the 5th. The big southpaw threw hard but was not a polished pitcher. Coach Wilson expected Trip to eat up some innings against the weaker teams during the season but not see much action in the crucial games.

With some work, Trip could be a good pitcher, Coach Wilson thought, as Trip retired the first hitter on four pitches. *Getting him to work during the offseason will be the problem . . . he's so committed to basketball . . . as he should be.*

The next hitter slashed a single to left, the next drew a walk, and Trip grimaced on the mound. He turned, looked at Rob at short and Buck Buckman in center, and heard their encouraging words. He nodded at them and turned back to face his next hitter . . . and then walked him on four pitches. Bases loaded. One out.

This brought Rob to the mound for a quick conference.

"Hey," Rob said quietly. Trip gazed back silently.

"We can't defend a walk," Rob continued. "You're trying to be too fine . . . you've got good stuff . . . trust it. Make em' hit it . . . you've got a good defense out here."

Trip nodded, set his jaw tight, turned back to the mound, and stared in at Bruce Smithers for the sign. He rocked his big frame back and threw his best fastball . . . the hitter swung and ripped a pitch into the hole between short and third.

The ball was by Josh Lee at third, but Rob dove headlong and speared the ball on one hop. It was hit so hard . . . and the runner at third was not very fast . . . so Rob hopped up and fired a strike to Bruce Smithers at the plate.

Smithers danced to the front of the plate as the runner from third headed home. He stretched out toward short like a first baseman to snag Rob's throw just in time to get the force at home. Two outs . . . bases still loaded.

The crowd went crazy! They took a deep breath. Top of the order coming up.

Trip rubbed up the ball and nodded in gratitude at Rob, who nodded back. He stepped up on the hill and again threw his best pitch . . . fastball out over the plate.

The Hillsdale crowd groaned as the ball exploded off the bat and headed for the gap in right-center field.

Trip's head snapped around as the ball looked to be sure to clear the bases . . . then . . . he saw Buck Buckman glide into the picture.

Buck was streaking toward the gap and closing ground quickly. Just as it appeared the ball would fall in and skirt to the fence, Buck dove full length and reached out his glove hand as far as it would go.

Ball meets leather. Buck squeezes. Hits the ground hard. Rolls over. Springs up. Holds his glove high. Shows the ball in glove. Inning over. Hillsdale's crowd explodes.

Trip trudged off the mound toward the first base dugout but turned and waited . . . first for Rob and Bruce, who he high-fived and thanked . . . and then for Buck Buckman.

When Buck reached the dugout, Trip grabbed his friend in a giant bear hug.

"Thanks, man! Great catch!" Trip yelled.

"Easier to play defense when they hit the ball," Buck answered. "Keep throwing strikes!"

"Will do," Trip answered with a laugh.

CHAPTER 6
MARCH-SOPHOMORE YEAR

*A***FTER** the first two hitters were retired in the bottom of the 5th, Gavin Ford laced a single to center. Buck Buckman slapped another hit, and Mark Porter walked, setting the table for Rob Mathews, with the score still 1-0 Braxton.

Again, the crowd ratcheted up the noise level, and Emily and Allison looked at each with hope . . . both saw Grandpa Russell had his rally cap on. They laughed, and he smirked.

"You know it works, girls," Grandpa Russell shouted over the crowd noise. "Watch and learn."

The Braxton coach knew he was in trouble . . . bases loaded, two outs . . . and nowhere to put Rob Mathews. He hesitated and made a decision . . . he was going to the bullpen.

In came a massive kid . . . Braxton's version of Hulk Thomas, and he was throwing heat.

Rob watched closely as the big kid warmed up, and he could see no finesse . . . simply raw speed . . . with the ball appearing to rise slightly as it reached the plate . . . no great movement.

"Come on, Rob! You can do it!" Allison heard herself scream.

"He will," Grandpa Russell shouted back. "He will."

The burly righthander on the mound checked the runners, reared back, and fired strike one across the heart of the plate.

Rob looked back at the mound. *He's fast . . . but that one didn't move that much. Four-seamer to get a strike,* Rob thought.

Ball one. Ball two. Two cutters. High velocity. Great movement.

Strike two. Fastball down Broadway. No movement. Four-seamer.

Ball three. Cutter. High and away. Great movement.

Rob stepped out and gathered himself. *He can't throw that cutter for a strike. Four-seamer down the middle,* Rob surmised as he dug in at the plate.

The big hurler again checks the runners dancing off all three bases. Peers in for a sign. Shakes one off. Shakes yes to the next one. Comes set. Fires home.

Four-seamer. Right down the middle.

Screaming line drive right over the pitcher's head. Two runs score. Hillsdale leads 2-1!

Grandpa Russell is beside himself, telling everyone close . . . and not so close . . . about the power of his rally cap!

Trip McHenry strides confidently to the plate. He had watched Rob's battle closely. He knew what to expect first pitch. *Cutter. The pitcher is not feeling confident about his four-seamer,* Trip thought. *Look cutter . . . but make sure it's a strike!*

First pitch. Cutter. High and away. Rob steals second. Two runners in scoring position. A chance to put the game on ice. Second pitch. Cutter. High and away.

I've got him now, Trip thought. *Here comes the four-seamer.*

Third pitch. Four-seamer right down the middle.

Popped up. On the infield. Third out. Missed chance to blow the game open.

The crowd deflated but quickly realized that Hillsdale had grabbed the lead. But, for some, like Grandpa Russell, there was the nagging feeling they had not cashed in. *Hope that doesn't come back to haunt us,* Grandpa Russell mused.

***

OUT came Rob to pitch the top of the 6th, and he sparkled on the hill, striking out a pair around a pop-out to first. He had used all his pitches and had a good feel for each one.

As Rob walked off the field toward the dugout, Braxton's first base coach stopped him, and Rob recognized him as one of Braxton's assistant basketball coaches.

"Don't suppose you'd be interested in moving into our district, would you, kid?" the coach drawled.

"No, uh, I'm, uh, set up here," Rob stuttered.

"Just kiddin', kid," he returned. "Kind of kidding . . . love to have you."

"Uh, thanks," Rob replied.

***

IN the bottom half of the 6th, Bruce Smithers and Toby Tyler started the inning with back-to-back singles, putting runners at the corners, and probably 15 followers of Grandpa Russell's rally cap were imploring the Pirates to add to their lead.

The hulking right-hander for Braxton realized he was at the bottom of the order and concentrated on throwing his four-seamer for strikes. He got Matt Bryant on a three-pitch strikeout for the first out.

Josh Lee stepped in . . . he had hit the ball well so far . . . and he did so again . . . smacking a hard grounder . . . right at the shortstop . . . who fed the second baseman, who made a clean, quick turn and nipped Josh at first for an inning-ending double play.

***

*N*OW it was Hulk Thomas time. This was the job Coach Wilson was grooming Hulk for . . . at least early in the season. *Come in, throw smoke for one inning, and close out the game.*

Rob had approached Hulk about coming to his house for some extra work on his pitching . . . but Hulk had not been too receptive. Coach Wilson had advised that they sit on it until next week, so Rob had not pushed it. Hulk looked great on Wednesday and Thursday at practice.

The skies were darkening as Braxton came up to hit in the 7th inning. Daylight Savings started this weekend . . . but today, the darkness was creeping in early. Hulk would be tough to see.

But . . . it didn't matter if they could see Hulk's pitches . . . because Hulk could not throw very many strikes . . . or maybe just not enough strikes.

He faced eight batters . . . and he struck out the side. But . . . he walked five . . . walking in both the tying run and the go-ahead run on 3-2 pitches.

Hillsdale was one strike away from a victory when a close 0-2 pitch was called a ball. Hulk went on to walk in the tying run.

They were one strike away from going to the bottom of the 7th tied when a close pitch was called a ball . . . and Hulk walked in the go-ahead run.

Hulk Thomas was seething on the mound because he hated to lose and hated to do poorly. When he came off the field after finally getting that last out, he was still seething . . . until he started sobbing . . . he was crushed.

The crowd was crushed as well. The Pirate's signature 2-1 victory over the powerhouse Braxton High Broncos had turned sourly into a 3-2 deficit.

"At least we have the last shot," Grandpa Russell bellowed. "On with your rally caps!!!"

Half the crowd good-naturedly followed suit, and Allison and Emily joined in . . . while Grandma Russell demurred.

The crowd lit up when Gavin Ford led off with a walk. A wild pitch advanced him to second, and Buck Buckman laid down the perfect sacrifice bunt to move him over to third . . . and beat the bunt out for a hit to boot.

"We are going to do it!" Grandpa Russell screamed. "Meat of the order coming up."

Buck Buckman promptly stole second on the first pitch, and the Braxton coach decided to walk Mark Porter to set up a force play at every base. But . . . that brought up Rob Mathews, Trip McHenry, and Bruce Smithers . . . all with chances to win the game for the Pirates.

"We're going to do this!!!" Grandpa Russell roared.

Allison Pierce winced. *Don't jinx us,* she thought. *Wait . . . since when did I get superstitious about sports? Oh, yeah . . . since I met Rob . . . and Grandpa Russell!!!!*

CHAPTER 7
MARCH–SOPHOMORE YEAR

*A*FTER a quick meeting on the mound, Braxton's Hulk Thomas "double" was removed . . . and on came Braxton's senior closer . . . an even bigger kid . . . who threw even harder!

Rob and Trip stood in the on-deck circle together and watched the big guy warm up.

"This guy's the real deal," Rob whispered to Trip as they watched the pitcher fire strikes with great movement into his catcher's glove.

"Yeah, but it only takes one of us to get a hit," Trip said. "Get er' done, "Wonder Boy!"

Rob smirked back at Trip.

"You don't want a chance?" Rob asked with a laugh.

"Nah, I'll let you be the hero," Trip laughed back. "Don't want to disappoint all of "Wonder Boy's" fans, now do we?"

Rob laughed again as the pitcher completed his warmups, and then Rob settled in to hit.

Strike one, called. Heater. With cut. Outside corner at the knees.

Strike two, called. Heater. With cut. Inside corner at the letters.

This guy is good, Rob thought. *Much better than the last guy.*

Strike three, swinging. Change up. Down and away. Rob way out in front.

The crowd groaned in disbelief. *Rob Mathews . . . a strikeout victim . . . in the clutch? What???!!!*

"This guy is tough," Rob said to Trip as they passed, visibly shaken at what had just happened. "Would like to have known he had that change. Hope you went to school."

"Yeah, I saw it," whispered Trip. "It was nasty."

In the crowd, Grandpa Russell was gaping at the field in dismay. He was at a loss for words. Emily knew she was in for a long night . . . and she was sad for her baby.

Allison was crushed. *No!!! Rob doesn't always come through,* she thought, *but he almost always does. He's going to be so unhappy. I feel like someone kicked me in the stomach . . . how does Rob feel?*

Trip McHenry stepped in, and the crowd rebuilt its noise level. Hillsdale still just needed one hit to win it . . . a sac fly to tie . . . anything.

First pitch. Fastball. Crushed to right field. Home run distance.

The big crowd erupted. Held its breath. Exhaled in disappointment. Game-winning grand slam foul by three feet.

Second pitch. Changeup. Popped up to short. Two outs.

Trip McHenry walked glumly back to the dugout. Disappointed in himself. The crowd disappointed as well.

Bruce Smithers' turn. A mature, confident senior. Seen it all. Played tons of travel ball. Poised. Clutch. *My turn to win it,* Bruce thought confidently.

The crowd was roaring, beseeching Bruce to come through. Hillsdale's dugout was on its feet doing the same. It felt like a playoff game or a league championship.

All through the crowd and the dugout, the same thoughts were racing through multiple heads . . . *we've got to win this . . . we have to pull it out . . . come on, Pirates . . . do it!!!*

First pitch. Cutter. Outside corner. Swinging strike one.

Gavin Ford, Buck Buckman, and Mark Porter screamed from the bases. Coach Wilson shouted encouragement. The bench was rocking, as were the fans in the bleachers.

Second pitch. Cutter. Down and in. Swinging strike two.

The scene repeats. The place is chaos . . . especially for a meaningless preseason game.

Bruce Smithers steps out . . . collects himself. *Look for the change,* Bruce thinks. *No . . . no, can't look for it, or he'll throw the fastball by you. Got to look fastball . . . but be aware of the change. Come on . . . throw me that change.*

Third pitch. Change up. Down and away. A swing . . . and a little flare heading into no man's land down the right field line. Gavin Ford is home . . . Buck Buckman is right behind him.

Foul ball . . . by inches.

The crowd explodes. Groans. Cries out, "NOOOO!!!!"

Everyone is standing. No one is breathing. Bruce Smithers is back in the box.

Gavin Ford, Buck Buckman, and Mark Porter are all back on their bases, ready to move on contact.

Pitch number four. Four-seam fastball. Above the letters. Above the hands. Blows Bruce Smithers away. Swinging strike three. Game over. Braxton 3-2 winners.

The air was let out of the crowd . . . and out of the Hillsdale dugout . . . and out of the Braxton dugout, as they exhaled in great relief. This was not a game Braxton was supposed to lose! They had escaped . . . just barely . . . just like in basketball.

CHAPTER 8
MARCH-SOPHOMORE YEAR

***C**OACH* Dave Wilson gathered his troops in the dugout after walking the line to shake hands with the Braxton players and coaches and was surprisingly upbeat.

His players, on the other hand, were reacting a little differently. Rob, Trip, and Bruce were berating themselves for not coming through . . . and feeling bad they had let the team down.

Hulk Thomas had stopped sobbing but was visibly shaken and still had the odd tear running down his cheek.

"Guys, you battled hard," Coach Wilson began. "That is a good team over there . . . an outstanding team."

The team heard him . . . but were not in the mood for a pep talk.

"Look, sometimes you lose because you were not the best team," Coach Wilson continued. "That was not the case today, though . . . you are right there with those guys. Sometimes, you lose because you don't prepare, or you don't put out your best effort . . . that was not the case today either . . . you all . . . all . . . tried your best."

With that, Coach Wilson scanned the dugout . . . engaging guys with his eyes, staying confident and positive.

"We missed a lot of opportunities today," Coach Wilson went on. "We had chances . . . chances to score . . . chances to close them out . . ."

Hulk Thomas popped his head up at that last comment and looked directly at Coach Wilson, tears flowing freely again.

"And, if I had to do it all over again," Coach Wilson said emphatically, "I would make the same decisions I made today again . . . with the same hitters in that position . . . and the same pitchers."

Hulk Thomas whimpered again but felt better hearing that last comment. He stopped crying and wiped his eyes dry.

"It's a learning experience, guys . . . today we learned that sometimes even our best efforts aren't good enough," Coach Wilson said. "You have to give it to that last pitcher. He is nasty. One of the best high school pitchers I've seen . . . and probably the best pitcher we'll face all year."

The team mumbled in agreement.

"But we have to learn from our mistakes or our shortcomings," Coach Wilson finished up. "We have to work a little harder . . . prepare a little better . . . get better at our weaknesses. We're right there, guys . . . we put in the work on the process of getting better . . . and everything else takes care of itself. OK . . . great game today . . . we'll see you Monday at practice!"

With that, the team started to scatter to gather their gear and head home for the weekend.

Rob, Trip, and Buck sat next to each other on the bench, still shaking their heads in disbelief.

"We should have won that thing!" Rob said softly.

Trip shook his head in disagreement.

"We blew it, man," Trip bellowed. "Bases loaded . . . no outs . . . and we can't at least tie it! I was pitiful."

"You were?" Rob retorted in derision. "You almost hit a game-winning grand slam . . . I couldn't even touch the ball . . . I'm the one who blew it . . ."

"No, I am!"

The trio popped their heads up.

It was Hulk Thomas.

Hulk wiped the last remnants of tears away and repeated himself. "No, I am!"

The guys looked at him, and Hulk suddenly had a massive scowl on his face. His competitiveness was coming into play . . . "I'm sorry, guys . . . I blew it," Hulk said sternly, berating himself. "And I don't like it."

The guys all nodded in agreement.

"Rob, I blew you off . . . you helping me with my control and learning new pitches and stuff . . . and I'm sorry. Coach is right about preparation . . . I thought I was ready . . . but I'm not . . . I have to get better."

"We all have to get better," Rob said sincerely.

"That offer to work out with you at your house still there?" Hulk Thomas asked with some hesitation.

Rob looked up at Hulk and smiled.

"You bet! See you tomorrow?" Rob asked.

"Name the time . . . and I'll be there," Hulk answered.

"How's 11:00 am?" Rob asked.

"See you then," Hulk replied as he stalked out of the dugout.

All three players turned and smiled. *That's a good sign,* they all thought.

CHAPTER 9
MARCH-SOPHOMORE YEAR

***A**LLISON* Pierce smiled as she gazed at Rob Mathews, Hulk Thomas, and Coach Dave Wilson in Rob's yard, or the "Auxiliary Practice Facility," as Rob had started to call it.

"Pretty big word for a jock," Allison had teased Rob the first time he called it that.

"Auxiliary or Facility?" Rob asked, taking the bait.

"No . . . Practice . . ." Allison said, melting Rob with her best smile.

"Hilarious, Allison," Rob returned. "I'm not sure why I like you!"

***

SATURDAY morning, promptly at 11:00, Ethan "Hulk" Thomas knocked on Rob's door, and the extra practice began. Coach Wilson had joined in about 30 minutes later . . . about the time that Allison had found an excuse to visit Emily Mathews . . . and get a better vantage point to watch Rob teach.

He's such a natural teacher, Allison realized. *He's patient, kind, helpful . . . and he explains things so you can understand them . . . well . . . at least "spooorts" things!*

Allison turned to Emily to find her quietly pondering the same thing. *Or was she?* Allison wondered. *She looks like she's watching Coach Wilson the same way I'm watching Rob! Hmmm.*

Emily felt Allison staring at her and turned and looked like she had been caught red-handed. *She was watching Coach,* Allison confirmed.

"He's such a good coach, isn't he, Emily?" Allison asked.

"Who? Rob? Oh, yeah, he is," Emily replied, clearly flustered at being caught.

"No . . . I meant Coach Wilson," Allison smiled at Emily.

"Oh, yeah . . . uh . . . he is . . . uh, too," Emily stammered.

Allison laughed softly and gave Emily a knowing look.

"It's all right, Emily . . . Coach Wilson is a cool guy," Allison said. "You two are a good fit."

"What, oh, no . . . uh, no . . . no . . . I'm not ready yet," Emily sputtered.

Allison smiled broadly, showing Emily her braces but trying to let her know it was fine.

"Well, uh, ok," Emily finally admitted. "I was kinda' watching him . . . and have been . . . he is a . . . he is a good guy. When I'm ready, he might be a good fit."

"Oh, Emily, I'm so happy for you," Allison gushed.

"Wait a minute, Ally," Emily protested. "I'm not ready and, well . . . who knows what might happen."

Allison stayed silent and glanced out at the guys.

"He is a good teacher, though," Emily conceded. "And a good coach. I find myself seeing Rob's father in him . . . he coaches in a very similar way . . . he cares about the kids and about how they will turn out as people, as adults . . . he reminds me of Jack."

Emily sniffled a bit and choked back the urge to cry.

"I'm sorry, Emily, I didn't mean to . . ." Allison said, seeing Emily was upset.

"Oh, no, I'm fine," Emily replied, regaining her composure.

"I'm also thinking how much Rob is like his Dad," Emily added. "He has that same soothing voice . . . kids really believe that he believes in them . . . it's a gift."

"Coach Wilson is like that, too," Allison said with authority. "In the classroom . . . I see it . . . and Rob talks about how he sees it too, in sports."

"Yes, Rob thinks a lot of him," Emily agreed. "I wonder how Rob would react if I dated Dave at some point?"

"I think he'd be fine," Allison answered quickly. "He really looks up to Coach Wilson."

"Ah, but if he's dating his Mom . . .?" Emily laughed.

"Yeah, you have a point," Allison replied with a snort.

"When do you think you might be ready?" Allison pressed.

"Oh, not yet," Emily quickly answered. "Once I'm ready to date . . . well, I'll call him and let him know."

"I hope he's not taken," Allison said lightly.

"Me, too," Emily answered with an embarrassed laugh.

"I see Ms. Fletcher, the science teacher, flirting with him sometimes," Allison said. "He seems to like her . . . but they aren't dating or anything."

Emily looked surprised but didn't comment.

They both peered back out at the guys, carefully reworking Hulk's pitching motion fundamentals.

Suddenly, Hulk threw a pitch to Coach Wilson, who was catching, and both Rob and the Coach exploded toward Hulk, pounding him on the back and praising him.

"I think he just did something right," Allison said, stating the obvious. "But I sure don't know what it was!"

Emily and Allison burst out laughing as Hulk stepped back on the mound and repeated the remarkable feat . . . and received another round of compliments. Next, he reverted to his old style . . . and Rob gently guided him back on track.

Emily and Allison both smiled at that.

"Dave Wilson and Amy Fletcher, huh," Emily mused aloud. "Cute couple."

"But not as cute as you and Coach," Allison said with a grin.

Emily smiled wistfully at Allison.

"Always the matchmaker . . ." Emily finally said to Allison.

"I try . . . and you can see how successful I've been with Rob!" Allison quipped, and they both laughed hard.

"So, now it's your turn," Emily said directly to Allison. "How is your plan coming with Rob? I still don't think he's ready yet, you know!"

"I'm afraid you're right," Allison lamented. "Right now, he says he's off girls for a while. I suggested he actually know and liked the girl before he went out with them . . . you know . . . know he likes them instead of just thinking they are hot."

Emily burst out laughing, and Allison joined her.

"I think I'll wait until junior year . . . maybe senior year . . . maybe he'll be mature enough to date a geek like me by then," Allison ventured.

"Oh, Allison," Emily replied with empathy. "You are not a geek . . . you are going to be one great catch for anybody with any sense . . . but . . . I'm not sure Rob has enough sense yet!"

They smiled warmly at each other.

"So, do you have a "friend" in mind for Rob to date in the meantime?" Emily asked, putting air quotes around the word "friend" with her fingers.

"Well, actually I do . . . and it's in Ms. Fletcher's science class!" Allison said brightly. "It's Lisa Cruz."

"Hmmm, I don't think I know Lisa," Emily answered. "Is she new in town?"

"No . . . I've known her for a while . . . she's a junior, though," Allison said.

"Oh, that's probably why . . . I don't know a ton of juniors," Emily responded. "Is she nice?"

"Nice . . . funny, smart . . . good looking, but not drop-dead gorgeous . . . but not ugly like me . . ." Allison said.

"Allison . . . stop putting yourself down," Emily said firmly.

"Anyway," Allison continued, "she's cute, a little shy around the guys . . . unless she knows them . . . and she knows Rob well. They are always kidding each other and talking a lot in science . . . especially since I got her assigned as lab partners with Rob and me!"

Allison broke into a satisfied smile, and Emily grinned back.

"You are a matchmaker, aren't you, Ally?" Emily smiled.

"Yes, ma'am," Allison retorted. "Sure you don't want me to work on Coach Wilson for you? You don't want to miss your chance!"

"Not yet," Emily said with an embarrassed smile. "I'll let you know . . . if and when I need help."

CHAPTER 10
MARCH-SOPHOMORE YEAR

*T*HE next three weeks let Rob Mathews know he was not in for a relaxing, walk-in-the-park baseball season . . . at least not this year.

Not only were there six preseason games to get through before league would start, with practices every day there wasn't a game . . . but Rob was working overtime at his house with Hulk Thomas . . . and several other teammates who loved coming by to hit in his cage, work a few infield drills, or just plain hang out.

On top of that . . . he and Trip McHenry were both taking driver's training classes in hopes of getting their driver's licenses in May when they both turned 16 years old!

As if that wasn't enough, Trip had another new girlfriend already . . . and was bugging Rob to go on a blind date with her friend!

"No, thanks," Rob stated emphatically on Sunday's "Movie Night" with Allison and her Mom. "I'm done with blind dates for a while!"

Allison and Trip rolled their eyes and laughed, but Rob was steadfast.

"Give him a few weeks," Allison whispered to Trip. "I'll wear him down."

***

EVEN with all that going on, the focus was definitely on baseball.

The Pirates bounced back from their heartbreaking loss to Braxton with a convincing 12-2 win over the Wolves from down in the Valley. Hillsdale's bats were booming, and clutch hitting was not needed . . . they scored early and often and ended the game in five innings.

Hulk Thomas got the last inning on the mound and was impressive. He struck out the side, allowing just one walk, but his new motion had certainly helped him stay balanced . . . and helped him find the strike zone much more consistently.

Coach Wilson had directed Rob to work first on getting Hulk to consistently throw the ball to his spots with the four-seamer before moving on to more advanced pitching.

"I'm afraid Hulk might have some hard times in the next couple of games . . . these next two teams are on a par with Braxton," Coach Wilson explained. "I don't think Hulk will be ready to add the cutter until after we play them . . . these good hitters might light up his four-seamer."

"Maybe we should just not pitch him against those two teams," Rob offered.

"No," Coach Wilson said, pausing as if in thought. "I think Hulk needs to get the picture that he will not be able to just blow people away with his four-seamer. Until he really sees that . . . I'm not sure he'll be receptive to working on the cutter and the change yet . . . I'm afraid he's going to have to feel some pain first . . . then we build him back up before league."

Rob nodded in understanding.

And Coach Wilson had been right. The first game saw a tight pitcher's duel, with Trip McHenry starting and going the first two innings, allowing just one run . . . a good solid outing. Rob had twirled the next four innings and also allowed a run.

Offensively, against quality pitching, the Pirates reverted to being unable to get that one big hit. They had 12 baserunners over seven innings but could manage just one run.

Coach Wilson handed the ball to Hulk Thomas for the top of the 7th, with the Pirates trailing 2-1. Hulk, throwing nothing but four-seam fastballs, was fantastic in throwing strikes . . . in fact, over five batters, he only threw two balls. The problem was those strikes were plastered all over the field . . . five screaming line drives . . . three for hits . . . but one for a huge double play that helped Hulk stay unscored upon.

His inning looked fine in the boxscore . . . but that didn't tell the whole story . . . he had been hit hard.

In the bottom half, Hillsdale got the tying and winning runs on base . . . but Toby Tyler flew out, and the Pirates dropped another heartbreaker by a 2-1 score.

***

*O**VER* that first weekend, Rob continued his work with Hulk, which was paying off. Hulk began to "spot" the ball where he wanted it with his four-seamer.

"You want me to show him the cutter yet?" Rob asked Coach Wilson on Saturday.

"No, let's wait until after Tuesday's game . . . I don't want him confused going up against Wainwright on Tuesday . . . they are tough," Coach Wilson answered.

And, tough they were. Their starting pitcher was big and strong and threw a variety of curves and changeups that had Hillsdale off balance. However, at the same time, he was hittable . . . except in the clutch. When the Pirates got baserunners . . . and they had a ton, Wainwright's pitcher would come up with the pitch he needed to get out of trouble. He stranded ten baserunners over the first six innings without allowing a run.

Brad Wallace had been nicked for a run in the first and threw a scoreless second. Jose Rivera came on and dazzled Wainwright with four nearly perfect innings . . . a walk and bloop hit being the only blemishes on his record.

The offensive frustration was nearly boiling over, and the Pirates were facing another one-run loss when suddenly, with two outs and no one on, Buck Buckman slashed a single, and Mark Porter followed with a double. Wainwright's closer wisely walked Rob to load the bases, and Trip McHenry finally came through with a single to center that scored a pair and gave Hillsdale a 2-1 lead.

Now it was Hulk Thomas time . . . the perfect setup for him to blow hitters away with his newfound control and overpowering fastball.

It was not to be . . . and it was over all too quickly.

The first batter slammed the second pitch into center for a single. Hitter number two turned on Hulk's third pitch, on an 0-2 count, and ripped a double into the left-field corner, tying the game. Batter number three hit a rocket off the fence in right on the first pitch, and the guy from second waltzed home with the game-winning run . . . and Hulk Thomas was in tears.

Coach Dave Wilson was suspiciously fine with the outcome . . . almost as if he hoped it would happen. He smiled when he pulled Rob aside as they boarded the bus for home.

"Now, he's broken down," Coach Wilson said in a whisper. "Tomorrow, we start building him back up . . . and we add the cutter."

Rob nodded.

"Do you think he's ready for it?" Rob asked.

"I think today taught him that he needs it," Coach Wilson said. "Before today, he didn't believe that."

"Good . . . I'm tired of losing like that," Rob laughed.

"Me, too," answered Coach Wilson. "The next three teams are weak . . . I'm going to get him a couple of innings a game. He won't need his cutter against these three . . . but it will be a good time to get some game experience. And, once he has the cutter down . . ."

"The change?" guessed Rob.

"The change!" replied Coach Wilson with a smile.

CHAPTER 11
MARCH-SOPHOMORE YEAR

C*OACH* Wilson wasted no time in building Hulk back up. During the bus ride home, he made three quick calls. Well, two quick calls and one a little longer.

The first two were to Hulk's folks and Trip's Aunt Barb. The last one . . . the one that lasted a little longer, was to Emily Mathews.

Rob watched as Coach Wilson zipped through the first two very professionally . . . and watched as Coach Wilson lingered a little longer talking with his Mom . . . hemming and hawing through the call like a teenager.

Hmmm, Rob realized. *Maybe Coach has the same trouble I do talking with hot girls he likes. Good to know I'm not the only one that has that problem.*

Coach Wilson's calls were to make sure he could have a quick meeting with the three players once they arrived back at school . . . and to let them know he'd drop them off at home as soon as they were done.

As soon as the bus arrived and the gear was unpacked, the quartet headed for Coach Wilson's office, and the three boys all grabbed chairs and sat facing the Coach across his big oak desk.

As they were settling in, the players admired the walls adorned with photos of Dave Wilson from his football playing days in high school and at the University of Southern California. *He was a stud athlete,* the boys all thought. *Probably still is!*

"OK, guys," Coach Wilson began. "Let's make this meeting quick . . . I don't want to keep you from getting to your homework!"

The guys grinned at Coach, and he returned the smiles.

"Hulk, let's get right to the point," Coach Wilson said, facing the young freshman pitcher. "You can't survive against the good or great teams if you only throw the four-seamer!"

Coach Wilson watched closely as Hulk's face started to crumple.

"And that's what we're here to talk about," Coach Wilson added quickly. "Getting you a couple of other pitches to compliment that fantastic four-seamer of yours."

Hulk battled and regained his composure.

"Trip, this applies to you as well . . . that's why you're here," Coach Wilson continued. "Your fastball is top notch . . . but you need to develop an off-speed and another pitch to be effective."

Coach Wilson could see Hulk relax, knowing he wasn't the only one.

"You guys will overpower the weak teams with your four-seamers . . . but as was shown the last couple of games . . . these great hitters eat four-seam fastballs for lunch," Coach Wilson stated. "You both need a fastball with more movement and an off-speed pitch . . . a slow curve or maybe a change up to mix speeds . . . but also to alter sight lines."

All three players nodded in agreement.

"Hulk, you've seen what Rob has done for you already . . . just getting your motion balanced and in control," Coach Wilson said. "You are throwing way more strikes and hitting your spots. Now I want Rob to teach you the cutter. Trip, the same for you."

The boys all nodded again.

"With the cutter, you will still be throwing harder than almost anyone out there . . . but you'll have movement . . . going both in and out," Coach Wilson added with a smile.

"Once you have that movement and control it . . . those hitters can't just sit on a straight fastball in a specific location."

"You think . . . you think I can learn it pretty quick?" Hulk asked tentatively. "We've only got three more games until league."

"It will take you a little bit," Coach Wilson answered. "You might pick the grip and stuff up quickly . . . but learning to control it might take some time."

Hulk nodded. "Think I can throw it this Friday?" Hulk asked.

Coach Wilson paused and pondered. He looked at Rob, who shook his head slightly.

"No, no, I think Friday we'll stick with the four-seamer . . . you should be able to power it by those guys," Coach Wilson finally said. "First, I want you to be confident you can throw that four-seamer where you want it when you want it. We'll have you work every day on the cutter and have you start throwing it in games next week."

Hulk nodded in agreement, smiling slightly.

"I think you're going to pick it up fast," Rob chipped in. "By next week, we can throw it in games, and when league starts, you should be comfortable throwing it all the time."

"I think both of you will pick it up right away," Coach Wilson agreed, including Trip.

"After you get the cutter down, we'll move on to a change," Coach Wilson continued. "That will take longer . . . but come playoffs, you'll have it down . . . and the combination of the four-seamer, the cutter, and the change will make you darn near unhittable!"

Hulk Thomas beamed at the Coach.

"Honestly," Coach Wilson said, "if you work hard with Rob on this . . . well, you can be an elite pitcher . . . not can be . . . will be an elite pitcher."

Hulk sat up a little straighter and smiled a little brighter.

"OK . . . let's head home," Coach Wilson said, standing and heading toward the door.

***

"**C**OACH, do you really want me doing all that work on pitching?" Trip McHenry asked after they had dropped Hulk at his house.

"Well, yes and no," Coach Wilson answered. "I know baseball's not your priority . . . and you are probably number-five on the pitching depth chart."

"Probably not that high," Trip snorted.

"Don't sell yourself short, Trip," Coach Wilson replied quickly. "You could be great . . . especially if you focused solely on that . . . but we both know that's not going to happen."

"You got that right," Trip replied, and they all laughed.

"But," Coach Wilson continued, "you'll pick up the cutter, and it will make you a better pitcher . . . one I can use against a good team. The change will also make you better . . . but let's get a feel for how you take to it before we spend a bunch of time on the pitch."

Both boys nodded in agreement.

"I appreciate you coming tonight, Trip . . . it made it easier for Hulk to hear when I didn't single him out," Coach Wilson added. "That's why having you work on the cutter too will help . . . plus . . . you were probably going to be over at Rob's anyway. You might as well be working out . . . right?"

"Yeah, right," Trip laughed. "You know me . . . always have to work my hardest at everything I do."

The trio laughed as they pulled up to Trip's house.

Trip hopped out and then leaned back in to share one last thought.

"Yeah, gotta' go 150% every second . . . don't want to fall behind "Wonder Boy," here!" Trip exclaimed with a laugh.

CHAPTER 12
MARCH-SOPHOMORE YEAR

THREE days later, Rob padded his way down to the kitchen to find, as usual, Grandma and Grandpa Russell perched at the dining room table with his Mom, enjoying Saturday morning coffee, breakfast . . . and the *Hillsdale Express* Sports Section.

"There he is," Grandpa Russell spouted as Rob slid groggily into a seat across from his Grandpa. "You ready to do some driving this afternoon?"

"Yeah," Rob said, suddenly wide awake and excited. "Sounds great!"

"What time is baseball done here?" Grandpa Russell asked.

"About 2:00," Rob replied.

Grandpa Russell gave Rob and thumbs-up and smiled over at Emily.

"Trip up for driving again today, too?" Grandpa Russell asked, and Rob nodded yes in response.

"Dad . . . are you sure you want to take on that responsibility?" Emily asked. "You know, I can teach Rob, and Barb is OK with teaching Trip."

"No, I love it. Besides, I'm getting to know Trip better . . . he reminds me so much of his grandfather, Chuck. And, it will be fun for me . . . and for the boys!" Grandpa Russell exclaimed.

"Fun?" Emily asked dubiously. "Somehow, I don't remember my driving lessons as fun."

"That was different," Grandpa Russell teased. "I don't expect to be pushing my foot through the floor to try to put on the brakes . . . or grabbing the steering wheel . . . or . . ."

"OK, that's enough," Emily said, laughing at her Dad. "I wasn't that bad."

Grandpa Russell just stared at her in disbelief.

"OK, maybe I was . . . but that was a long time ago," Emily said sheepishly. "Why don't you read Rob the "Old Grump" column from today?"

"Trying to change the subject, dear," Grandpa Russell said with a devilish grin.

Emily waved him away as the whole table laughed softly.

"Ahem, let's see . . . oh, here it is," Grandpa Russell said as he rustled through the sports section to find Dan Mercer's column.

"It's too early to tell what kind of baseball season we will get from Hillsdale this year," Grandpa Russell read. "The early returns have been hard to read. Explosive hitting followed by a team-wide lack of clutch hitting has hurt against the three quality teams Hillsdale has played . . . all losses, by the way. But . . . they were three excellent teams, and all were one-run losses. We got so used to seeing clutch hitting last year from Bill Tompkins, Bruce Smithers, Rob Mathews, and who can forget that unlikely hitting hero . . . Kenny Johnson!"

"Oh, I remember those hits," Rob said.

"Me, too," echoed Emily as Grandpa Russell nodded his agreement.

"The pitching has been very strong, especially from Rob Mathews and Jose Rivera. Brad Wallace and Trip McHenry have been solid . . . Wallace a little more polished and McHenry a big, strong, flamethrower," Grandpa Russell continued, pausing to smile at the mention of Rob's name.

"But the wildcard so far has been freshman Ethan Thomas. Better known around town as Hulk Thomas, the big right-hander has been overpowering at times . . . only to look like a batting practice pitcher against the good teams. He's blown two saves and looked like he was putting it on a tee for hitters in another game . . . but absolutely dominated in his other outings . . . including an awesome performance yesterday when he struck out three straight hitters on just ten pitches . . . ten straight four-seam fastballs."

"That's his problem," Grandpa Russell crowed. "Has he picked up the cutter yet, Rob?"

"Yeah, he really picked it up quick," Rob enthused. "He had no clue where it was going the first day . . . but it has great movement . . . I think he'll throw it next Tuesday if he does well today and Monday. The "Old Grump" say anything else?"

"Just one more comment," Grandpa Russell answered. "I understand from our own Dylan Cobb that Dave Wilson has Rob Mathews working with both Hulk Thomas and Trip McHenry on the cutter. Word is it is going well . . . but it's early in the process. Prediction time . . . if Hulk Thomas learns the cutter, he will be a force . . . if he learns a cutter and adds an off-speed pitch . . . well, it could mean Sectional Title time for the Pirates. You read it here first!"

"Ugh," Rob snorted. "I hope Hulk doesn't read that . . . and take it the wrong way . . . that's a lot of pressure on a freshman."

Emily smiled at Rob ruefully, remembering his eventful and pressure-packed freshman year. *Yes, if anyone knows about pressure as a freshman . . . it's you!*

CHAPTER 13
MARCH–SOPHOMORE YEAR

***H**ILLSDALE* had blasted their Friday opponent 16-1 and had two more preseason games before Spring Break . . . with League play starting after the break.

Spring Break also meant something special to Rob and his Grandpa Russell . . . Opening Day for their beloved San Francisco Giants . . . and a treasured family tradition.

"So, Rob," Grandpa Russell said as they walked from Rob's house to the Russell house to pick up Grandpa's car for Rob and Trip's driving lesson. "Opening Day is a week from next Tuesday . . . you guys don't practice, right?"

"Right," Rob replied with a grin. "Did you get tickets yet?"

"No . . . not yet," Grandpa Russell countered. "I have a line on some though . . . but wanted to see if you minded some company this year?"

"Company . . . ?" Rob asked warily.

Grandpa Russell waved his hand. "Oh, don't worry . . . you'll like this company."

"Who . . . ?" Rob asked, still wary.

"Well, Grandma for one . . . your Mom for another," Grandpa said with a smile.

"There's more . . . ?" Rob asked.

"I can get up to six tickets," Grandpa smiled. "Bleacher seats in left . . . second row."

Rob smiled. *The bleacher seats are cool,* he thought. *Bring my glove and nab a home run!*

"So, who are the other two?" Rob pushed for an answer.

"Well, I was thinking Trip and Buck!" Grandpa said with a grin.

"That would be awesome, Grandpa!" Rob replied enthusiastically.

"Thought you might not mind that," Grandpa Russell answered.

"Oh, ugh, uh, Buck is going to be out of town," Rob lamented. "He leaves next Saturday and gets back that Tuesday night late . . . some travel ball thing."

"Oh, too bad . . . Trip's in town?" Grandpa Russell asked.

Rob nodded.

"Well . . . who shall we ask . . .?" Grandpa Russell said.

Rob paused, and the first thing that came to mind shocked him.

"How about Allison?" Rob asked.

"How about her?" Grandpa Russell said. "She's a great idea! She enjoyed the game last year . . . and, well, going to her first Opening Day . . . she'll love it!"

Trip was in immediately . . . and so was Allison after she cleared it with her folks.

"I can't believe he asked me to go," Allison gushed to Emily after the boys were out of earshot. "I'm so excited!"

"About the game, right?" Emily asked with a sly grin.

"Oh, yes . . . just about the game . . . Rob's not ready to date yet!" Allison grinned.

Emily and Allison both laughed hard.

"Still, he did think about me, and that's a start," Allison said dreamily as Emily smiled.

***

As expected, the Pirate's next two games were blowouts. Tuesday's game was 12-0, and Friday's clash ended up 9-0. Hillsdale's pitching was superb... Brad Wallace and Jose Rivera had thrown two impressive innings each in the first game, and Hulk Thomas the last two... the game ending after six innings because of the 10-run rule.

Hulk had unleashed his new pitches... as he threw a cutter that would go both in and out... and he threw it effectively. Mixing it with his four-seamer, he struck out five but walked one in each inning. His command of the strike zone was not there with the cutter yet, but he overpowered his opponents and felt great about his performance.

Friday's game saw Trip, and Rob, split the first four innings, with Hulk going the last three. Trip's cutter looked good, although he struggled to throw it where he wanted. He allowed one hit and a walk, while Rob was perfect in his two innings.

Hulk came out and looked confident and ready. He threw three almost perfect innings ... allowing just one baserunner on a 3-2 count walk with his cutter. However, he also used his cutter two other times in 3-2 counts... and both times got strikeouts.

After the game, Hulk was elated... and so was Coach Wilson.

"Guys... you looked great out there," Coach Wilson enthused. "Hulk... you are a different pitcher... and going into league... well... we're the team to beat!"

The team responded with a cheer.

"Now, remember," Coach Wilson concluded. "You have the weekend off... and Monday and Tuesday. Wednesday, be ready to come back in and work hard. First league game is a week from next Wednesday. Enjoy your break!"

Trip and Rob smiled at each other.

I know I'm going to enjoy mine, Rob thought. *Opening Day, here I come!*

CHAPTER 14
APRIL-SOPHOMORE YEAR

*T*UESDAY couldn't get here fast enough for Rob. Sunday and Monday were spent working with Hulk and Trip on their cutters. Sunday was also "Movie Night" with Allison and Trip. The rest of the time was spent bantering feverishly with Trip on who was the better franchise . . . the Giants . . . or the hated Los Angeles Dodgers.

Having grown up in L.A., Trip was a diehard Dodgers fan . . . Rob was a diehard Giants fan . . . and the two teased and constantly bickered now that it was baseball season.

"Aw, you're nuts!" Trip scoffed at Rob. "The Dodgers have won five world series since they've been in California . . . they're the best."

"Aw, you're nuts!" Rob lashed back. "All of those were before you were born! When was the last one . . . 1988! My Mom was just a kid!"

And, so it went . . . back and forth. Always with a smile . . . but also always serious!

The pair went through their routine on the trip to "The City" for Opening Day at the Giants' beautiful stadium by the Bay. For Trip, it was his first visit to the stadium . . . and while duly impressed, he wasn't about to give Rob anything.

"Yeah, pretty nice stadium," Trip said mid-way through the game.

Rob rolled his eyes. "Pretty nice? I suppose you're going to tell me that Dodger Stadium is better?"

"Absolutely," Trip responded, and off they went. "You ever been there . . . ever had a Dodger Dog?"

"A Dodger Dog?" Rob scoffed. "Sounds like dog food! You've had enough food today to know this is better than a Dodger Dog . . . it's actually edible!"

"Aw, you're nuts!" Trip exclaimed with a playful scowl.

The game was a good one. Well played, nip and tuck, with Opening Day electricity coursing through the stadium.

Rob sat between Allison and Trip and enjoyed the banter, the view of the park, and the game on the field. Rob also marveled at Allison. *She is becoming a real fan,* Rob thought. *She knows what she is talking about . . . her sitting next to Grandpa Russell has really paid off!*

As the game wound down and got tight, it was Allison who spouted out some advice for the Giants' manager.

"Time to bring in the closer," she said. "If there was ever a time for a four-out save . . . well, this is it!"

Rob did a double-take, and then he looked at Trip, who was amazed . . . and then past Trip to Grandpa Russell, grinning broadly.

"That's one smart cookie," Grandpa Russell crowed. "She's a student of mine, you know!"

Allison beamed proudly and smiled at Grandpa Russell.

The Giants manager must have been listening because in came the closer to get out of the 8th inning. He was back for the ninth to close out a scintillating 4-3 victory for the Giants, and the group left happy . . . even Trip . . . who stopped to buy one last tidbit from the vendors for the road!

CHAPTER 15
APRIL-SOPHOMORE YEAR

*A*FTER the game ended, they piled back into Grandpa Russell's Minivan for the long ride home into the Foothills. Grandma and Grandpa Russell were in the front seats, Allison and Emily in the middle row, and Rob and Trip sprawled out in the back.

They listened to the post-game radio show, relived the highlights, and then settled back for the ride home.

"So, what are your summer plans, Allison?" Emily asked after the radio was turned off.

"Oh, I'm going to have some fun this summer!" Allison exclaimed.

"Do tell," Emily replied with a smile.

"Well, right when school ends," Allison began, "maybe even a day or two before school ends . . . our whole family is taking a trip to Europe!"

"Europe, oh, how exciting," Emily said. "That will cost your folks a pretty penny!"

"Well, not too bad," Allison replied. "You know my oldest sister works for United Airlines. We're flying "Standby," so the tickets will be next to nothing."

"How great," Grandma Russell commented. "Europe is magical."

"And, we have relatives in England . . . so we're staying with them." Allison continued. "And, they have friends living in France . . . so we're all staying with them!"

"Oh, Allison, that sounds great!" Emily said enthusiastically.

Hmmm, Rob thought as he listened, *that means Allison will be gone while we are . . . so she'll be around to hang out the rest of the summer.*

"But that's not the best part," Allison gushed. "After we get back, I'm heading straight to my sister's place in San Francisco and living with them for the summer! And . . . I'm working at my middle sister's Summer Camp . . . well, she works there, too . . . it's not her Summer Camp. Zack is going to work there, too!"

"Oh, Allison, that's so nice," Emily said.

"Who's Zack?" Trip asked.

"He's a guy I met last year in San Francisco," Allison replied. "He lives near my sisters."

Well, that changes the summer, Rob thought. *Wait a minute here . . . I don't hang out with Allison much in the summer . . . why does that not feel good? Is it because Zack is working there? What???*

"I get to work with kids all summer," Allison continued. "Camp ends just a day or two before school starts . . . I'm gone all summer!"

"Wait," Rob spoke up, "I thought you loved Hillsdale . . . you said you'd always want to live here!"

"Oh, I still do . . . I would never leave Hillsdale for good," Allison returned. "But this is going to be so much fun . . . living with my sisters and working with kids!"

"How about you, Trip?" Emily asked.

"Well, oddly," Trip answered, "I'm going to be working at a Summer Camp, too."

Rob snapped his head around to face Trip.

"Wait, what?" Rob asked. "When did this come up?"

CHAPTER 16
APRIL-SOPHOMORE YEAR

"*THIS* will be my second year," Trip replied. "My Dad set it up for me . . . working at the USC basketball camp . . . pretty much from July 1st to the first week of August . . . I'll be back in time for football practice, though."

Now, Rob was whirling. *Trip is gone, too. What am I going to do?*

"Yeah, it's a pretty sweet gig," Trip laughed. "Play hoops all day . . . and get paid for it. Going to need some cash when I get a car, you know."

"Oh, Rob . . . that's what you should do," Allison piped up.

Now it was Emily's turn to snap her head around . . . at Allison. *NO! Rob can't leave for the summer . . . he's just a baby.*

Emily turned back to Rob, who had a half-smile on his face. *Uh, oh,* Emily thought. *He's thinking about it.*

"Do you think there is a job for Rob?" Allison asked Trip.

"Might be," Trip drawled. "They were still looking for a couple more guys. But I thought Rob was gone on a baseball trip for a while."

"Well, we are," Grandpa Russell interjected. "But we are back by July, aren't we, Robby?"

"Yeah, we get back June 29th," Rob answered, suddenly hopeful. *This could be a great summer!*

"Do you think I'd have a shot?" Rob asked Trip.

"I think so!" Trip answered excitedly. "Let me text the guy right now. I've known the guy who runs it for a long time . . . he's friends with my Dad."

"Whoa, wait a second here," Emily finally found her voice. "I need a little more info. Like where would you be living . . . and who is supervising you?"

Trip laughed, and the rest of the car joined in . . . except Emily and Grandma Russell . . . who were both in Mom mode.

"They've been running this camp forever," Trip said. "I went as a little kid. The counselors all stay in the campus dorms and have adults supervising. We dorm with the kids during the week . . . and then just the counselors and adults on the weekends . . . don't worry, it's safe."

Emily looked skeptical but could already see that Rob would push for this to happen.

"OK," Emily said slowly. "Find out if there is a spot . . . but I want to see the information on the camp . . . and talk to the guy who runs it before I say yes."

"YESSS!!!" spouted Rob loudly. "That would be so cool!"

With that, Trip started texting furiously, and they all anxiously awaited an answer.

"Say, Rob . . . Trip . . . I was just thinking," Grandpa Russell said loudly, to be heard in the back. "Trip, would you like to join us on our baseball trip in June?"

The car turned completely silent.

"Do you . . . do you really mean it?" Trip finally said, breaking the silence.

"Yes," Grandpa Russell smiled. "You girls won't mind, will you?"

Emily and Grandma Russell looked at each other.

"Well, no . . . I wouldn't mind," Emily said without hesitation.

"Me either," said Grandma Russell, turning and beaming at Trip. "Emily and I are only going on about half the trip."

"Well, Mom . . . I might be going for longer if Rob is going to be gone the rest of the summer," Emily said, with a slight pout on her face.

"Where all are you going this year?" Trip asked.

"Rob, you fill him . . . you planned it," Grandpa Russell said proudly.

"Doing the Midwest this year," Rob said with a grin. "Starting in Minnesota, then Kansas City and St. Louis . . . after that, we head to the Chicago area and see the White Sox, Cubs, and the Brewers in Milwaukee."

"Wow!" Trip said appreciatively.

"We're not finished," Rob continued. "Next, we go to Cincinnati, Detroit, Toronto, Cleveland . . . and finally, we finish up in Pittsburgh!"

"Wow!!!" Trip exclaimed. "That is amazing!!!"

Now it was Allison's turn to feel left out. *I wish I could go with them*, she thought. *Wait! Who am I kidding? I'm not that big a baseball fan!*

"Are you really serious, Grandpa Russell?" Trip asked.

"Absolutely!" Grandpa Russell replied. "You'll have to pay most of your own way, of course. But we can talk to your Dad and Aunt Barb about that . . . Rob is paying for some of the trip himself, too . . . from whatever he made at his summer job . . . so maybe that can be a part of it, too."

"I'm in if you'll have me!!!" Trip exclaimed.

"Then you're in!" cried Emily.

Trip's phone buzzed . . . and Emily looked at Trip.

Trip bent over and read out loud:

"I've got one spot left. I'll email you all info. Your word on this guy is good enough for me. Need to know by first thing in the morning. Shall I hold the spot?"

Emily froze. She looked at Rob. Stared him down. *Oh, my baby. He wants this bad. I have to let him. He deserves it. I can trust him. Can I trust everyone else?*

Rob gazed back at her with pleading eyes.

"Do you want to do it?" Emily finally asked Rob.

He nodded in reply.

Slowly she looked around the car. Grandpa Russell caught her eye in the rearview mirror and smiled his assent. Grandma Russell turned around and smiled as well. Allison was quiet, but she, too, looked at Emily and smiled.

Emily turned to face the boys . . . who both broke into wide grins.

"OK . . . OK," Emily finally said with a small laugh. "A tentative yes . . . until I've read the material and talked with the boss."

"YEAH!!!!" Trip and Rob called out in unison.

The boys fist-bumped, Trip turned to his phone and texted quickly: ***"Hold it!!!"***

Trip turned the phone screen so Emily could see . . . she looked for a long moment . . . and then nodded.

Trip hit "Send," and the boys exploded in cheers.

Summer, here we come, Rob thought as he cheered. *But first, we have a baseball championship to win!*

CHAPTER 17
APRIL-SOPHOMORE YEAR

OPENING Day of any sport, in any season, is always special. For Rob, even the last two years at Hillsdale High . . . when he had to sit and watch his teammates play instead of being on the field . . . were still special. The adrenaline flows . . . and there is just something extraordinary in the air.

But . . . Opening Day of league play . . . when you are the reigning League Champs . . . and you have old teammates in the stands . . . well, that takes it to another level!

Warming up his arm, Rob scanned the bleachers and spotted his Mom and Grandparents, Trip's Aunt Barb and her kids, and Allison Pierce and her Mom. *That's a surprise,* Rob thought. *Mrs. Pierce doesn't come to baseball games too often . . . I guess everyone thinks this is a special occasion.*

Rob continued scanning and saw Stephanie Miller, her steady boyfriend Phil Boyer, Donnie Fields and Christina Craft, and a host of other friends from football, basketball, and school.

His eyes found last year's teammates, Bill Tompkins, Scott Harper, and Kenny Johnson, standing with Coach Dave Wilson in front of the dugout. *It is great to see those guys,* Rob mused, not realizing how much he had missed Bill and Kenny.

The loudspeaker broke into his thoughts as the announcer blared out, "Now, for the raising of the League Championship banner . . . here is Coach Dave Wilson, and three alumni who are back in Hillsdale to help us celebrate today . . . Kenny Johnson, Scott Harper and . . . Bill Tompkins!!!"

The crowd rose as one and serenaded the trio with an overwhelming chorus of cheers. The boys soaked it in, tipped their Hillsdale Pirates caps, and moved to the flag pole to help hoist the flag high above the field behind home plate.

Rob was choked up . . . suddenly remembering Kenny Johnson's home run to beat Pine Bluff for the League Championship . . . and the party the town had after that game. *Priceless!*

He gazed over at Kenny Johnson and remembered how much that hit had meant to him. And, how much it meant to Bill Tompkins and Scott Harper to finally . . . finally . . . get that championship banner.

As quickly as the ceremony had started . . . it was over . . . and the trio of alumni left the field amid a huge ovation and numerous back slaps, fist bumps, and high-fives from current players and fans alike.

Rob got the shivers from the excitement of watching the championship banner snapping at attention in the gentle breeze. The large crowd let out a giant roar, and Rob just let it soak in.

Hopefully, we can do this again next year!

Now . . . it was game time.

CHAPTER 18

APRIL-SOPHOMORE YEAR

*T*HE Milltown Miners were Hillsdale's Opening Day assignment. Milltown, a perennial powerhouse in most sports, was again putting a solid team on the field.

Junior Jose Rivera got the ball on the mound after finishing the preseason on a high note, and the Pirates took the field to a massive roar from the crowd.

In his first Varsity league game, the young southpaw came out blazing, throwing three straight fastballs, before getting Milltown's leadoff hitter to strike out on a nasty slider in the dirt. A routine grounder to third baseman Josh Lee got him the second out on one pitch.

Milltown's number three-hitter scorched one up the middle, but Rob Mathews ranged far to his left, did a 360 behind second base, and fired to first . . . where he nipped the baserunner at first by an eyelash, aided by a great stretch by towering Trip McHenry at first base!

With that, the Pirates bounded into the dugout amidst thunderous applause from their fans and got down to the business of scoring runs.

It didn't take long.

Buck Buckman led off the game with a screeching double into the left-center field gap. On the next pitch, Mark Porter ripped a single to center, and it was 1-0.

Rob Mathews followed with a double off the left-field fence to make it 2-0. Rob promptly stole third and scored on a Trip McHenry sac fly, putting Hillsdale up by three.

The offense stalled after the sac fly, but Jose Rivera retired the Miners in order in the top of the 2nd, and Hillsdale was back in business in the bottom half.

Josh Lee got things going with a one-out single to right field. Gavin Ford followed with a tricky grounder into the hole between short and third, and both speedsters made any play impossible for the shortstop.

After Jose Rivera popped out, Buck Buckman smashed a solid shot into the 5-6 hole. Milltown's shortstop fielded the ball with a slick backhand but looked up to see Buck flying down the line. He unleashed a wild throw over the first baseman's head and off the fence into short right field.

When the dust settled, Buck was at third, and both Josh and Gavin had scampered home, and it was 5-0. Mark Porter took a called third strike, and the inning was over.

Hillsdale's Rivera continued to deal in the 3rd and 4th innings, allowing his first hit in the 3rd and a walk in the 4th, but got through both innings unscathed.

The Hillsdale offense sputtered in both innings. They got hits from Rob and Trip to start the 3rd, but Bruce Smithers, Matt Bryant, and Josh Lee could not get the big hit to cash in on the opportunity.

In the 4th inning, Gavin Ford continued his hot hitting with another single with one out. Jose Rivera bunted him over, but Buck Buckman was finally retired on a liner to second base.

Rivera found himself in his first real trouble in the 5th inning, when back-to-back singles with one out put runners at the corners.

This is where the strong defense of Hillsdale came into play. On Rivera's first pitch, the number nine-hitter slashed one toward the right-field corner. At the last second, Trip McHenry went into basketball mode and climbed the ladder to rebound the line drive in the web of his big first baseman's glove.

In the stands, Trip's Aunt Barb and his cousins went crazy. Grandpa Russell high-fived them both, grinned at Allison, and gave her the thumbs up.

What came next was even more impressive. The Miner's leadoff hitter ripped one up the middle. Mark Porter dashed to his right, backhanded the ball, and shoveled it to Rob floating by . . . using just his glove. Rob was waiting for this . . . having worked with Mark on the play during "extra practice time" at his house.

Rob caught Mark's shovel, already in throwing motion, and threw a strike to Trip at first.

"YOU'RE OUT," shouted the umpire, and the Hillsdale fans went bonkers.

Rob and Mark were pummeled as their teammates came off the field, and Jose Rivera gave them heartfelt high-fives as they reached the dugout steps.

Milltown's coaches also went bonkers, as they were sure their runner had beaten the throw.

"No way," Allison crowed to Grandpa Russell. "He was out at first by half a step!"

Grandpa Russell just grinned at her and winked at Emily.

"That girl is going to be a keeper," Grandpa Russell whispered to Emily.

Emily shushed him and turned to see Allison grinning ear to ear.

"I hope he's right," Allison said happily to Emily, who smiled in return.

CHAPTER 19
APRIL-SOPHOMORE YEAR

***H**ILLSDALE'S* offense went 1-2-3 in the bottom of the 5th, and in the top of the 6th, it was apparent that Jose Rivera was running out of gas.

He struggled with the first hitter, going to a 3-2 count, before finally getting him on a fly ball to Buck Buckman in center. Milltown's number three and four-hitters followed with two rockets to left for hits, and Milltown had life.

Rivera buckled down to induce an unassisted force out at third, but the Miner's number six-hitter roped a single to left, and Milltown was on the board, with the score standing 5-1 in favor of Hillsdale.

The Hillsdale fans were getting restless.

"We can't let this one get away," Grandpa Russell said with concern. "Better get Hulk ready."

"I think Coach Wilson heard you," Allison piped up, motioning to Toby Tyler and Hulk Thomas, who were scurrying down to the Pirates bullpen.

"Thank goodness," Grandpa Russell sighed.

Rivera continued to labor, walking the next hitter on four pitches to load the bases, and Coach Wilson popped out of the dugout in a hurry.

"How you feeling, Jose?" Coach Wilson asked as soon as he got to the mound.

"I'm a little tired," Jose began, "but I really want one more hitter . . . I know this guy . . . and I know I can get him."

Coach Wilson looked Jose in the eye . . . then gazed over at Rob, knowing he would have an opinion.

Rob nodded his head slightly.

"I think Jose's got this guy, Coach," Rob said firmly. "He's made him look bad both times today."

Coach Wilson nodded in agreement and gazed at Jose intently.

"OK . . . you deserve this," Coach Wilson said. "You've pitched a heck of a game. One more hitter."

Jose smiled wearily, but his face turned into a hard mask as he stepped back onto the mound, and his defense reset.

Two straight balls had Coach Wilson worried . . . and thinking about going back to the mound. *Can he do it?* Coach Wilson wondered. *Is he done?* He searched Jose's face from a distance. *Determination and confidence . . . that's all I see . . . that's enough for me.*

Strike one. Strike two. Nasty slider on the 2-2 pitch. Strike three swinging. Inning over . . . and so was Jose's day.

Jose was mobbed as he came off the field, and Coach Wilson met him with a bear hug.

"Great job, Jose," Coach Wilson said. "Gutsy pitching."

But this one wasn't over. The Pirates squandered a scoring chance in the bottom of the 6th, and Hulk Thomas made his way into the game as Milltown came to the plate in the top of the 7th.

Hulk started the inning with a four-pitch strikeout, showing excellent command of his four-seamer and the cutter.

That turned the lineup over to the top of the order, and Hulk threw five good pitches to Milltown's leadoff hitter and got the pesky lefty to rap into a groundout, Mark Porter at second to Trip McHenry at first.

Then things got a little sticky. Hulk seemed to lose focus, and his control of the cutter went with it . . . a four-pitch walk.

"Uh, oh, don't give them hope," Grandpa Russell lamented.

Up came Milltown's best hitter . . . and he didn't disappoint.

Hulk threw him a cutter for ball one. A cutter for ball two. A four-seamer straight down Broadway . . . fouled straight back, and Hillsdale breathed a sigh of relief.

"Got away with that one," Grandpa Russell shouted.

A cutter for ball three and a 3-1 count.

Four-seamer.

Bye, bye, baby! Score: 5-3 Hillsdale.

The crowd was now really restless as Hulk Thomas went back on top of the mound.

A four-pitch walk. All cutters.

The Hillsdale crowd murmured uneasily. Coach Wilson was on the top of the dugout steps . . . *should I talk to him? Get him out of there . . . or not?*

Rob Mathews headed to the mound. Coach Wilson stopped.

Let's let Rob handle him . . . he is Hulk's pitching coach . . . he knows more about it than I do, Coach Wilson realized.

Rob got to the mound and could see panic starting to rise in the young freshman hurler.

"Relax, Hulk. Trust your stuff," Rob began, exuding calm, confidence, and relaxation. "Focus on the glove . . . don't grip too hard . . . just throw the cutter for strikes. They won't hit it."

Hulk looked at Rob warily.

"Believe it . . . you got great stuff," Rob said with a smile. "Relax, focus, and throw your cutter for strikes. Game over."

Hulk nodded, and Rob trotted back to his spot at short.

Tying run at the plate. Two outs.

First pitch. Cutter. Outside corner. Strike one.

Second pitch. Cutter, On the knees. Inside corner. Swinging strike two.

Third pitch. Cutter. Right down Broadway.

Great movement. Swinging strike three. Game over.

Hulk let out a massive sigh of relief . . . just like the everyone else in Hillsdale green and white.

CHAPTER 20
APRIL-SOPHOMORE YEAR

"**C'MON,** Rob!" Trip McHenry whined. "Why not?"

"You want me to go out on a double date with you and Kathy Thigpen . . . and who?"

"Tasha Phillips," Trip answered. "C'mon, you know her . . . hot girl in our history class."

Sitting in the cafeteria with Rob, Trip, Buck, and Toby Tyler, Allison Pierce wrinkled her nose at the term "hot girl."

Rob knew Tasha well . . . *slender, long legs . . . blond and beautiful.*

"Tasha doesn't date guys in our class," Rob countered, knowing she usually dated guys that were Juniors or Seniors.

"Well, she told Kathy she'd date you, "Wonder Boy!" Trip laughed. "I know, I know, hard to believe, but it's true!"

The group cracked up, including Allison.

"Well, she is really hot," Rob conceded, weakening his stance . . . until he caught Allison glaring at him. *This is what she is always talking about,* Rob realized. *I'll go out with anyone hot . . . whether I know her or like her or not!*

"Then I can tell Kathy it's a date," Trip pushed.

"I'll go with you if he won't," Toby Tyler interjected enthusiastically.

The group cracked up again . . . except Allison.

"You guys are awful," Allison said loudly, rising from her seat.

The guys all looked stunned.

"Only dating girls that are hot," Allison continued, her anger growing. "When are you guys going to learn it's not all about looks?"

"Oh, Ally, we just . . ." Toby started, but Allison cut him off.

"No, it's crazy . . . not everyone can be "hot" . . . but who are people like me going to date if all you guys will only date "hot" girls," Allison spouted angrily. "You guys are jerks!"

The table went silent.

"And I can tell you, Rob Mathews . . . when I'm hot, I'll **NEVER** date you . . . because I know all you care about is looks," Allison vented, pointing her finger at Rob and then turning and stomping off.

The table stayed silent for a long time.

"Yeah, like Allison Pierce is ever going to be hot," Toby Tyler smirked.

Trip, Buck, and Rob all looked at Toby, realizing they did not like the sound of the comment.

"Just kidding . . . just kidding," Toby said defensively, taking note that the comment was insensitive.

"So, how about it, Rob?" Trip persisted.

Rob paused and looked around the table at the guys, but he didn't see Allison return and stand right behind him.

"Nah," Rob finally said to the guys. "I'm gonna' pass, Trip. Tasha and I have nothing in common . . . she's nice and all . . . but it would kinda' be like Stephanie Miller. If I'm gonna' date, I want to date someone I can really talk to . . . you know . . . about interesting stuff . . . not art or music . . . or clothes."

"Ah, man . . . then find a date . . . you can still join us," Trip implored. "It'll be fun!"

The "end of lunch" bell sounded, blocking out the last part of Trip's words, and they all got up to head off to class.

Rob turned around and was startled to see Allison standing right on top of him.

"Oh, uh, hey, Allison," Rob stammered. "Thought you were long gone."

"I was," Allison conceded. "But . . . I came back to apologize . . . it's none of my business who you date . . . but . . ."

"But, what?" Rob asked.

"But . . . I'm proud of you for saying no to Trip," Allison gushed. "And for saying what you did . . . you're getting smarter."

"Yeah, well . . . thanks to you," Rob admitted.

They turned to head to class . . . their shared Science class was next, and they hung back a bit from Trip, Toby, and Buck, who were all in the class as well.

"So, with that newfound maturity, are you ready to have me set you up with Lisa Cruz?" Allison queried.

Rob wrinkled his nose in exasperation.

"She's a junior . . . why would she want to go out with me?" Rob asked, going over the ground they had covered before.

"Because she likes you . . . duh . . ." Allison laughed. "That's the usual reason."

Rob frowned at her in disbelief.

"She does, Rob . . . you guys are always talking and laughing," Allison added. "You're always having fun in class. Plus, she's a "jockette" . . . you have "spooorts" in common!"

Rob pondered those comments. *She is an athlete,* Rob thought. *We do joke around a lot and she's fun to be around.*

"Is it because you don't think she's hot enough for you?" Allison demanded.

"No . . ." Rob started.

"Because I've seen her when she dresses up," Allison powered on. "I saw her at Homecoming this year . . . with makeup and her hair done . . . she looked great! Of course, you weren't at Homecoming . . . again! You know, you still owe me a Homecoming Dance!"

Rob smiled at Allison's remark and nodded.

"Next year, I promise," Rob laughed. "Was Lisa at the Sadie Hawkins dance?"

"No, she's too shy to ask anyone," Allison replied. "You see . . . she's kinda' like you . . . she's really friendly and fun if she is comfortable . . . but shy and awkward if she doesn't know you . . . just like you!"

"Shy and awkward . . . me???" Rob protested with a smile.

"Shy and awkward . . . at least," Allison laughed. "Cringe-worthy is more like it!"

They both laughed as they reached their class, filed in with the rest, and found their seats.

Allison looked over across the room and saw Rob looking at her. She flashed him her best smile, and Rob returned it. *Good deal . . . glad that fight is over,* they both thought.

Rob's mind wandered back to Allison's short tirade, which made him really think. *What if Allison were hot? Would I date her then? In a minute. So, why shouldn't I date her now? Maybe I am a jerk! She's smart, funny, a great friend . . . we can talk forever. Maybe I should ask her out. Would she says yes? Maybe not . . . she said she'd never date me if she was hot . . . but she's not hot. Should I date Allison? Nah, not Allison. But why not?*

CHAPTER 21
APRIL-SOPHOMORE YEAR

*A*s class ended, Rob realized he had daydreamed away the whole period. He was slow in getting up to head to his next class, and when he hit the hallway, he spotted Allison Pierce and Lisa Cruz walking down the corridor, deep in conversation. *What are they talking about?* Rob wondered.

"No, I really do think he likes you," Allison was busy telling Lisa at that moment.

"Really?" Lisa answered in surprise. "I sure can't tell... I mean, we talk and joke around ... and it's fun ... but he's never come close to asking me out or anything!"

Allison spit out a short burst of laughter.

"Rob? Ask you out?" Allison laughed. "You'll be lucky if he ever asks you out... or ever asks any girl out. He's just brain-dead when it comes to talking with girls."

"But he talks to me all the time ... and to you," Lisa protested.

"That's because we're safe ... and he knows us," Allison explained, while Lisa looked skeptical.

"I'm just his geeky next-door neighbor ... and certainly not hot," Allison explained. "You're a Junior ... and for some reason, that makes you off limits in Rob's mind ... but it also makes you safe. No way you will date him ... so he can be himself."

"Hmmm," Lisa replied slowly. "I get it, Allison ... he's really shy ... I'm like that, too."

"That's why you guys are perfect for each other," Allison continued. *What am I doing this for?* Allison screamed at herself. *Why am I always trying to set him up with other girls? Right, oh that's right . . . if I can get him to date a normal girl like Lisa, maybe he'll notice me . . . as long as Lisa doesn't become Mrs. Rob Mathews!*

"Well, maybe . . . I do kinda' like him," Lisa said. "He is a nice guy . . . not like a lot of the other jerks in this school."

Allison started to tell Lisa about their lunchtime scene in the cafeteria but paused. *She won't want to hear the "hot" part of that discussion.*

Allison turned to say goodbye as they parted company for different classes. As they smiled their goodbyes, Allison really looked at Lisa. She was about five-foot-five, with a slender but strong, athletic figure . . . she was a starter on the Varsity Volleyball team this year. Her dark brown curls fell to her shoulders, and her complexion contrasted Allison's pale tone.

Interesting, Allison thought. *Lisa never wears makeup, and yet she's cute . . . pretty, even . . . but not hot. She doesn't dress flashy . . . almost tries to hide that she is cute. But at Homecoming . . . she looked gorgeous . . . not like Stephanie Miller or Tasha Phillips . . . or Carly Neel! But . . . she's pretty . . . I hope setting them up doesn't backfire . . . I hope someday Rob Mathews is mine.*

CHAPTER 22
APRIL-SOPHOMORE YEAR

H**ULK** Thomas peered intently down from the mound on Saturday at the Mathews "Auxiliary Practice Facility," or the "APF," as the gang had started to call it lately.

The name had come out of a conversation in science class Wednesday afternoon between Rob, Buck, and Trip . . . with Allison and Lisa Cruz listening in . . . and putting in their two cents!

"So, you coming over to the "Auxiliary Practice Facility" Saturday to throw?" Rob asked Trip. "Hulk's coming over at 11:00 am . . . you can throw after him. . . I know you need your beauty sleep."

"Yeah, you're one to talk about beauty sleep, "Wonder Boy," Trip cackled. "But I'll take the Noon slot . . . I do like sleeping in . . . sometimes!"

"What in the world is the "Auxiliary Practice Facility?" Lisa Cruz asked incredulously.

"Oh, it's what we call the practice area at my house," Rob replied quickly. "We have a small practice infield . . . a full-sized batting cage . . . a mound we built . . . you know . . . a real practice area."

Lisa's face dropped, then grew wary.

"You're putting me on, right?" she grinned.

"No, unfortunately, he's not," Allison chimed in. "I've got stinky, loud boys outside my bedroom window all the time!"

The group laughed hard.

"So, do you always call it the "Auxiliary Practice Facility?" Lisa quizzed.

"Yeah . . . what else would we call it?" Rob asked. "That's what it is!"

"Quite a mouthful," Lisa laughed, staring at Rob.

"Big words for jocks, too," Allison added.

The girls laughed while the guys looked perplexed.

"So, what should we call it?" Trip prodded.

Lisa thought for a long moment.

"Well, the easiest would be "APF," Lisa finally said.

The guys stared back in puzzlement.

"You know . . . an . . . acronym . . ." Lisa explained slowly.

The guys continued with blank stares.

"You know . . . the initials . . . A for Auxiliary . . . P for Practice . . . and F for Facility," Lisa spelled it out. "Like the NBA, MLB . . . NFL . . . duh!"

The light had gone for the guys, and they immediately adopted "APF" as the official name.

"What a great idea, Lisa!" Rob grinned. "I like it . . . a lot!"

Rob and Lisa shared a smile . . . and Allison beamed at Rob. *Oh, geez . . . here we go . . . sometimes I think I'm too good a matchmaker! I may have just lost Rob!* Allison thought.

***

F*AST* forward to Saturday, and Hulk Thomas was at the end of his workout. Hulk had been very effective in his two innings on Thursday when the Pirates had demolished Foothill 12-0 in six innings in Foothill.

Hulk's control of the cutter had been sharp, and he had mixed the cutter with his four-seamer to strike out five of the six batters he faced . . . with the other guy grounding out weakly to Trip McHenry, unassisted at first base.

Hulk got an inning in an 11-2 rout of the Taylor Tornados on Friday. The starting pitching had been strong, and the offense was hitting on all cylinders. The entire lineup was contributing, with the 8-9-1-2 hitters setting the table for the meat to drive them in.

Today, Hulk's workout had also been sharp, and Rob was in the squat behind home plate as Hulk was finishing up. Trip McHenry was early for his workout . . . and was posing as a righthand hitter to give Hulk a better visual.

"All right," Rob yelled out. "Let's finish strong. Last batter. Bottom of the 7th . . . Sectional Championship against Valley Christian. We're up by one . . . bases loaded . . . two outs. Who do you want to face?"

Hulk didn't hesitate.

"That little weasel, Tony Russo," Hulk barked out.

Rob and Trip both smiled, knowing Hulk and Tony had crossed paths often in the youth leagues . . . with Tony winning most of the battles.

"I guess I better squat down a little," Trip drawled as he bent over to lower his strike zone. "That Russo's a little guy, isn't he?"

"Yeah, he is!" Rob shouted, aware that Trip knew Tony was about the same size as Rob.

"Guy's a jerk!" Hulk replied, and all three nodded.

Allison Pierce shook her head in her bedroom, overhearing the boy's remarks. *What's wrong with Tony?* she wondered. *Must be guy stuff.*

"OK, you know the situation . . . you know you hate the guy," Rob coached. "You've got to control your emotions . . . make quality pitches . . . and hit your spots . . . with movement!"

Hulk peered in, and Rob flashed the sign for a cutter down and out. The big kid took his time . . . fired a strike . . . knee high, outside corner . . . good movement.

"Strike one," screamed Trip McHenry.

Another sign . . . this time to the inside. Another strike. Inside corner, knee-high.

"Strike two," yelled out Rob.

Trip snapped his head back, playfully arguing the call and getting in Rob's face.

"All right, Hulk," Rob called out. "Focus. Relax. Throw me your best pitch, flashing the signal for a cutter back to the outside part of the plate.

Hulk took his time, gathered himself, let out a deep breath, reared back, and let it fly. The pitch was perfect . . . just below the knee, just off the plate an inch . . . almost unhittable.

Trip took a giant swing with his arms, and his "Tony Russo" went sobbing off the field.

The trio high-fived and went crazy, simulating their Sectional Championship.

Allison Pierce rolled her eyes. *Boys . . . I just don't get it!*

CHAPTER 23

APRIL-SOPHOMORE YEAR

"*ROB*, can you grab that," Emily said as her cell phone jangled during Sunday "Movie Night" while her hands were deep in a sink full of dirty dishes. "Just put it on speaker!"

Rob dropped the plates he was clearing on the counter, sidestepped Allison and Trip, who were right behind him, and stabbed the phone with his index finger to answer the call.

"Hello," Emily called out.

"Hi, Mrs. Mathews?" the voice said.

"Yes . . . what can I do for you?" Emily asked with a quizzical look on her face.

"This is Frank Parker from the USC Basketball Camp."

"Oh, hi, Mr. Parker," Emily replied. "Thanks for calling. What's up?"

"Absolutely, Mrs. Mathews," Frank Parker replied. "I just wanted to confirm that Robert's application to work at the Camp this summer has been accepted. We look forward to having him with us . . . we hear great things about him from Bill McHenry."

"Oh," Emily croaked out . . . a knot forming in her stomach. "That's . . . great!"

Rob and Trip silently jumped up and down and fist-bumped at the news.

"AWESOME!!!!" Rob mouthed to Trip, who fist-bumped him again.

"We will send you a packet with all the forms Robert will need . . . if you can please fill them out and send them back ASAP, we'll be all set."

"Will do," Emily squeaked out.

"Well, awesome," Frank Parker said. "We'll see Robert . . . and Bill in early July. Have a great night!"

"Uh, er . . . thanks," Emily managed.

This is happening, Emily realized. *A whole summer without Rob home. I guess I need to get used to that . . . he only has two more years of high school!*

Emily dried her hands, avoiding turning around as long as possible. Finally, she turned and saw Rob and Trip fist bumping and doing a little dance.

"Well," Emily said slowly, fighting back the tears, "I guess you have a job."

"Yeah!!!" Rob shouted while Trip echoed the thought.

Allison was torn. *I'm going to be gone all summer . . . why does this make me sad? I guess I feel bad for Emily.*

Rob noticed Emily's reaction.

"Mom, you OK?" he said in a low voice, coming toward her and reaching out his arms for a hug.

"Yeah . . . yeah," Emily choked out. "I guess I just didn't expect you to start heading off until you graduated."

Rob pulled her close.

"It's just a month or so, Mom," Rob said, starting to tear up himself.

"I know," Emily cried. "I know . . . I'll be OK."

Rob hugged her tight, not even aware of the other folks in the room . . . who were all watching closely . . . and feeling the situation.

"Well, I guess that makes one decision for me," Emily said, stiffening herself and smiling at Rob, Trip, Allison, and Allison's Mom.

"What decision?" Rob asked.

"I'll be going with you for the entire baseball trip," Emily laughed through her last tears.

"That will be great, Mom!" Rob said with genuine enthusiasm.

"You sure?" Emily asked uncertainly.

"I'm sure," Rob said quickly.

Emily looked around the room.

"You sure, Trip?" Emily asked.

"You know I am!" Trip answered immediately.

That's why I'm sad, Allison realized. *I want to be on the baseball trip instead of going to Europe . . . at least Emily gets to go with them.*

Emily smiled and pulled Trip in to form a three-way hug.

After a long hug, they moved toward the living room and their movie . . . with Rob and Trip still high-fiving . . . and Emily and Allison still sorting through their mixed feelings.

CHAPTER 24
APRIL-SOPHOMORE YEAR

*M*ONDAY afternoon, Coach Wilson called Rob and Hulk aside at the end of practice and asked them to stay late, along with reserve catcher Toby Tyler.

Rob knew what was coming . . . *time to add the changeup,* he thought with a smile.

And, so it was . . . as Dave Wilson corralled the trio into the bullpen and immediately told them the purpose of the extra session.

"All right, Hulk," Coach Wilson began. "You have made great progress in a very short time . . . must be a great student and a great teacher!"

Coach Wilson waved at Rob when he said that.

The boys laughed softly.

"Now Rob is going to teach you the pitch that is going to take you from being a pure power guy . . . to a guy that will be unhittable," Coach Wilson proclaimed. "The change!"

Hulk nodded . . . he knew this was coming at some point and was excited to get started.

"So, you've seen how your movement with the cutter . . . now that you are controlling it well . . . has pushed you into a higher level," Coach Wilson said, noting Hulk's look of satisfaction at the compliment. "Once you master the change . . . you're going to be in a class with that Braxton closer . . . an elite pitcher."

Hulk loved that compliment, and he puffed up with pride.

"Uh, thanks, Coach!" Hulk said, looking away sheepishly.

"But it won't come overnight," Coach Wilson said. "It's a real touch pitch . . . getting control can take time . . . I don't expect you to throw it in the first half of the league season . . . maybe not until the end . . . but we need to have the option come Sectionals."

Hulk nodded and looked at Rob.

"Which change you going to teach me?" Hulk asked Rob.

"We're going to start with the "Circle" change," Rob grinned back at Hulk. "It's a little tougher to learn . . . but if you can pick it up, I think it will be the best fit."

"Let's get started!" Hulk replied enthusiastically.

The first results were not overwhelming. Hulk struggled, and the ball squirted in every direction. Rob stepped in with some tips, and things improved slightly.

A few minutes later, another tweak helped, and the ball started looking like an actual pitch . . . as opposed to a three-year-old pretending to be a pitcher.

After about 50 changeups, Coach Wilson called it quits for the day.

"That's enough for today," the Coach called out. "It was a great start. Let's work it into the regular workout, Toby . . . and Rob, maybe you can give it some extra attention this weekend at the "APF.""

Rob grinned at Coach Wilson using the "APF" nickname.

"Will do, Coach," Rob returned. "I think the "Circle" is going to work for him . . . it's just gonna' take some reps!"

***

THE week was a busy one for the Pirates, with three more league games. On Tuesday, Hillsdale piled on their bus for the ride to Oakville to play the Acorns.

The Pirates jumped on Oakville for four in the first inning, with Toby Tyler driving in three with a bases-loaded double. Jose Rivera continued his hot pitching and dazzled Oakville through six innings, allowing just one run on four hits and a walk.

The Pirates picked up another pair of runs in the 5th, and Hulk Thomas lumbered in from the bullpen to close the Acorns out in style. Using his cutter extensively and with great location, he overpowered Oakville, striking out the side on just 13 pitches!

On Wednesday, Hulk threw the change in practice, which was passable, but the feel and location still had a long way to go.

Thursday, at home against a tough Barker City squad, Hulk was reminded why he was working on the change.

Hillsdale slowly built a 7-1 lead, scratching out two in the 1st, one in the 4th, two in the 5th, and their final runs in the bottom of the 6th. They had multiple chances to break the game open, but missed chance after chance.

Brad Wallace had gone five strong innings, and Trip McHenry bridged the gap to Hulk Thomas with a solid 6th inning.

With the big hometown Hillsdale crowd cheering them on, the Pirates looked poised for an easy win. Unfortunately, Hulk's recent pinpoint control of the cutter didn't show up for the game.

Hulk walked the first two hitters on 3-2 pitches, and felt he was getting squeezed by the umpire. His frustration grew as he went to 2-0 to the third hitter when two pitches he felt sure were strikes were both called balls by the ump. Hulk's head was swirling, and his temper was near the boiling point.

He peered in for the sign from catcher Bruce Smithers and shook him off until he got the four-seamer. He threw the pitch as hard as possible, right down the gut. *He's not gonna' be able to call this pitch a ball,* Hulk thought angrily.

And, the umpire didn't call it a ball . . . because Barker City's cleanup hitter quickly deposited the ball over the center field fence, and all of a sudden, it was 7-4.

Hulk was steaming mad . . . at the umpire and himself . . . and he tried to regroup.

"No worries," Rob Mathews said, approaching Hulk from his shortstop position. "Ump's been tight . . . take a deep breath and relax . . . relax your fingers . . . get the movement . . . focus on the glove. The strikes will come."

Hulk nodded, his anger subsiding. He turned back to climb onto the mound and was surprised to see Coach Wilson standing there.

"This is your game, Hulk," Coach Wilson said confidently, looking Hulk directly in the eye. "Relax . . . focus . . . I believe in you . . . so does the team!"

Hulk was overwhelmed. *Coach does believe in me. I can do this!*

Back to their places went the team. Hulk got back on the mound, and suddenly, the ump was not blind. The pitches he had been missing by inches were now catching the corners, and after the first few, Hulk's confidence soared.

Three hitters. Three strikeouts. Game over. Hillsdale on top 7-4.

Saturday, the Pirates overpowered Colton 14-2 in a game that lasted five innings. Trip McHenry went the first four, allowing both runs, but had a double, homer, and five RBI's at the plate. Hulk Thomas pitched a perfect inning to close it out.

"I really, really wanted to throw a change out there today," Hulk told Rob after the game. "I can feel it . . . I think it's ready to go."

Coach Wilson, overhearing the conversation, sidled over and said, "Let's just keep that under wraps until after the Pine Bluff game . . . we want to unveil the change in the second half . . . your cutter and four-seamer are looking great right now!"

Hulk nodded . . . but he wasn't happy. *I really want to throw that pitch in a game . . . now!*

The win left Hillsdale with a 6-0 record in league . . . with Cooley on the road Tuesday of next week . . . before a Thursday showdown at home . . . with the Pine Bluff Warriors.

Now . . . here comes the fun!

CHAPTER 25

APRIL-SOPHOMORE YEAR

"*H*ELLO," Rob said, answering the telephone Sunday morning.

"Hey, Rob, Dylan Cobb here," the caller replied.

"Hey, Dyl, what's up?" replied cheerfully.

"Did you hear about the Pine Bluff-Cooley game yet?" Dylan asked.

"No . . . wait . . . did Pine Bluff get beat?" Rob asked excitedly, pressing the speaker button so his Mom, Grandparents, and Trip McHenry could hear both sides of the conversation.

"No, afraid not," Dylan responded. "But, they almost did. Pine Bluff was down 1-0 going to the bottom of the 7th . . . and Cooley made two errors in a row that cost them the game."

"No way . . . Cooley?" Rob answered. "Are they that good? Or is Pine Bluff down this year?"

"Cooley's the real deal, Rob," Dylan replied with feeling. "You guys can't look past them. Their ace is tough . . . really tough . . . and the Coach told me he was throwing against us on Tuesday."

"Yeah, I remember him from last year," Rob said. "He was good . . . we eventually got to him . . . but it wasn't easy."

"Well, I just wanted to give you guys the inside info," Dylan said. "Don't look past these guys . . . or we might be sorry."

"Thanks for the heads up, Dyl," Rob said. "See you at school tomorrow."

Rob turned to the group and saw Trip with a grim look on his face.

"That guy's a lefty, right?" Trip asked.

"A tough lefty," Grandpa Russell remarked. "And, he's better this year . . ."

"Time to hit the batting cage?" Rob asked.

"Darn right," Trip said as he lumbered toward the kitchen door. "You got a left-handed machine out there?"

***

"So, how was your date with Kathy Thigpen last night?" Allison Pierce snarkily asked Trip McHenry. "Fireworks?"

Trip McHenry glared across the dinner table in Allison's dining room Sunday night and watched as Rob, Emily, and Linda Pierce leaned forward to get the report.

"No . . . no fireworks," Trip drawled in response. "If "Wonder Boy" here had come through and found a date, it would have been fine . . . but . . ."

The group laughed, and Rob turned red.

"But . . . let's be real here," Trip continued. "It's really Allison's fault Rob couldn't get a date . . ."

The group paused . . . not sure what Trip meant.

"Yeah," Trip cackled, "Allison's didn't ask anyone out for him . . . so how could he possibly get a date?!!!"

With that comment, the group howled... except for Rob, who half-smiled and felt his face get red with embarrassment.

"Hey, I'm working on it," Allison insisted with a smile. "Maybe a prom date..."

Eyes were raised around the table.

"Do tell," Emily said, looking at Rob.

"I don't know... what she's... talking about," Rob stammered.

"You know, Rob," Allison said coyly. "Lisa..."

Rob sat frozen.

"Lisa Cruz?" Emily asked.

"Yes," Allison replied. "I think she might ask Rob... I've been working on her."

"Well, that would be nice, Rob," Emily said slowly, feeling Rob's pain.

"I don't want to go to prom with anyone," Rob whined. "Besides... I'm just a sophomore... we aren't supposed to go to the prom. That's for juniors and seniors."

"You went last year as a freshman," Allison reminded him with a smile.

"That... that was different... I was helping out Dee Dee," Rob protested.

"Well, you would be helping out Lisa this year," Allison explained. "She wants to go, but no one has asked her... and you guys both like each other!"

"And you can help me out," Trip piped in.

"You???!!!" Rob asked with irritation.

"Yeah," Trip replied with a bemused smile. "I think I'm kinda' gonna' be helping out a junior that night, too!"

"Who?" Rob queried with growing dread.

"Jillian Parker," Trip smiled.

"Jillian . . . Lisa's friend?" Rob asked, suddenly understanding what was going on.

"It's perfect, Rob," Allison said with a huge smile . . . that, for once, did not melt him away. "You guys will all have a great time."

Rob looked back and forth between Allison and Trip.

"So, you're in on this, too, huh?" Rob asked, looking directly at Trip.

"In on what?" Trip objected. "I don't have a clue what you're talking about."

Trip looked down, obviously lying and not doing a great job of it.

"C'mon, "Wonder Boy," Trip grinned. "We've got to get our boy hero back in the saddle again."

Rob looked at the whole group dubiously.

"And, what's the worst thing that could happen," Trip continued. "We get a nice dinner out . . . the girls can drive . . . no parents . . ."

With that, Trip paused and winked at Emily, who was starting to react with mock panic.

"If it all goes bad . . . we've got each other," Trip finished sarcastically.

"Yeah . . . the two of you . . . dinner and dancing . . . what more could you want," Allison quipped devilishly.

"Aw, geez," Rob whined again. "Dancing . . . I'm going to need another dance lesson."

"You're going to need more than one lesson," Trip guffawed. "I've seen you dance!"

They all laughed hard again . . . except Rob, whose face turned three shades of red darker in embarrassment.

"I can help you again with that," Emily volunteered.

Rob looked at her, pleading with his eyes to get her to "stop helping."

"But . . . maybe . . . maybe you'd prefer to have Allison help you," Emily said slowly, an idea forming. "I'm getting kind of old . . . you know, out of step with today's dances."

Allison's face brightened as she immediately saw what Emily was doing.

Rob glared at his Mom. *Thanks a lot for helping, Mom,* he thought ruefully.

"I'd love to help you with that," Allison gushed.

Rob stole a glance at Trip, who was eating it all up. Trip looked back with a wicked smile.

Rob suddenly had a thought.

"This is all great planning," Rob pronounced. "But . . . Lisa hasn't even asked me yet . . . I can't go if she doesn't ask me!"

"I can help with that, too," Allison said lightly.

"Oh great . . ." Rob answered sourly. "Thanks a bunch for helping out."

"My pleasure," Allison replied. *I hope it's my pleasure in the long run. He better not fall for Lisa!*

CHAPTER 26
APRIL-SOPHOMORE YEAR

*T*HE Hillsdale Pirates piled out at the Cooley High field undefeated in league . . . and they were determined to stay there.

The weather had turned gray, with the chance of light showers predicted . . . but both teams wanted to get this game in. Especially Hillsdale, as they hoped to ride home with a chance Thursday to take control of the league standings with a win over Pine Bluff.

The Pirates were sending junior sensation Jose Rivera to the mound. The slender lefty had dazzled opponents all year and was the co-ace of the staff with Rob Mathews. Coach Wilson had opted to go with Jose today and Rob on Thursday against Pine Bluff.

Hillsdale was facing the standout pitcher in their league . . . Seth Gardner. Gardner, another lefty, had danced his way through the first half of the season sporting a minuscule 0.50 ERA and had suffered just the one gut-wrenching loss to Pine Bluff late last week.

The Pirates were accompanied to Cooley by a strong contingent of loyal fans, who sat huddled together, trying to stay warm on the third base side.

Grandpa Russell sat bundled up with his Pirates' hat stuck on his head. As usual, he sat with Emily and Allison Pierce and spoke confidently about how this game would end.

"We'll get by Cooley," Grandpa Russell said softly. "We always do. They will give us a battle . . . but we'll get them in the end. We beat them today, and they'll be out of the race completely . . . two games back . . . and Pine Bluff will be the only team to worry about!"

A battle is what Hillsdale got from Cooley.

Buck Buckman greeted Seth Gardner and the Cougars with a clean single to center on the game's second pitch. A Mark Porter sacrifice bunt moved Buck to second and brought up Rob Mathews . . . who was immediately given a free pass to first base.

That brought up Trip McHenry, who waged war with Gardner, forcing him to throw ten pitches . . . before finally lining out to second base.

Bruce Smithers was next . . . and instead of trying to work some more pitches out of Cooley's ace, he unwisely took a cut at a low and outside curveball on the first pitch and popped out to shortstop, stranding both Buck and Rob on the bases.

Jose Rivera came out and shone in the first inning. Working quickly, throwing strikes on the corners, and changing speeds, the young hurler got three quick outs on eight pitches.

Back to the mound for Seth Gardner, who immediately got into trouble by walking Toby Tyler and giving up a soft blooper to left for a single by Matt Bryant. That set the Pirates up with runners at the corners and nobody out.

Here is where Gardner had stymied Hillsdale last year in the early going of both games. With runners in scoring position, he seemed to find a more refined focus and made great pitches to escape multiple jams.

With Josh Lee at the plate, Gardner dazzled him with an assortment of off-speed pitches and got Josh to chase one in the dirt to strike out swinging.

The ball scooted away from the catcher, allowing Bryant to move up a bag, giving Hillsdale runners at second and third with one out.

Gardner dug in again and surprised Gavin Ford with an inside fastball on his second pitch and Ford popped it up to short. Two outs.

It was quickly apparent that the Cooley coach had done his homework as he flashed four fingers to his pitcher and catcher, signifying a free pass to Buck Buckman to load the bases for Mark Porter. Cooley was not about to let Rob Mathews or Buck Buckman beat them.

With the bases loaded, Gardner returned to his windup and quickly dispatched Porter and the Pirates on a lazy fly ball to center.

And, so it went, inning after inning. Jose Rivera put down the Cougars with relative ease, while Seth Gardner frustrated the Pirates at every turn.

Gardner stranded another pair in the third and a runner at third with one out in the 4th inning. He got out of a bases-loaded, one-out jam in the 5th and stranded two more in the 6th inning.

It wasn't that Hillsdale was killing the ball . . . they were drawing tough walks, getting some dink hits, and were the beneficiaries of sloppy defense by the Cougars. A slight drizzle had begun in the 3rd inning, and the ball was getting slippery.

On the other hand, Jose Rivera continued to dominate, retiring the first ten hitters he faced before allowing a hit and a walk in the 4th. A perfect 5th inning was followed by another single in the 6th . . . but Rivera was able to keep the game scoreless.

The frustration was building both in the Hillsdale dugout and in the bleachers.

The umbrellas came out after the 6th, and the crowd tried to stay dry, but their spirits were as damp as the weather.

"Are we ever going to score?" Allison Pierce whined. "We need to score and get out of this weather."

"I know," Emily agreed. "It's freezing out here . . . Mom was so right to stay home."

Grandpa Russell looked at them with disdain . . . but he felt their frustration, too. *Only one thing to do,* he thought.

"Rally Cap time!!!" Grandpa Russell bellowed for all to hear.

The fans nearby grinned through their frustration, and several of them followed Grandpa Russell and turned their caps inside out.

The frustration was deeper on the bench, and players were now stressing about coming through in the clutch. Mark Porter, Trip McHenry, Bruce Smithers, Toby Tyler, Josh Lee, and Gavin Ford all had chances to drive in multiple runs, and none could get that one big hit.

Now, it was the top of the 7th, and the Pirates sent Bruce Smithers to the plate to start the inning. The rain had intensified slightly, and the ball was getting harder to control.

"C'mon', Bruce!" the dugout and the fans screamed.

But Seth Gardner had other ideas and made short work of Smithers, getting him to pop out in foul territory down the first base side.

Toby Tyler was next, and the burly sophomore lit a flame with a solid single to right-center. Matt Bryant sacrificed him to second and set up a battle between Gardner and freshman Josh Lee.

Josh had not touched the ball all day, striking out in all three plate appearances. He had been completely baffled by Cooley's southpaw and had not looked good . . . at all.

First pitch.

Bunt.

CHAPTER 27
APRIL-SOPHOMORE YEAR

THE entire Cooley team was caught off guard . . . and reactions were slow. The ball trickled down the third baseline, and Josh Lee scampered toward first. Toby Tyler raced toward third, watching to see what the third baseman would do with the ball.

Cooley's third sacker raced in, barehanded the ball, juggled momentarily, and threw toward first on the run, hoping to nab Josh Lee to end the inning.

After juggling, the third baseman rushed his throw, and the ball slipped slightly in his hand as he let it fly . . . he immediately knew he wanted the baseball back. His hand went to his head in fear, and he said a silent prayer that the first baseman would save the day.

The throw dipped crazily to the left and down, and the first baseman tried in vain to come up with it cleanly. The ball squirted off his glove and dribbled a few feet away as Josh Lee raced through the bag.

Toby Tyler was off on contact and never stopped running! He kept his eyes glued to Coach Wilson and heeded his frantic arm signals to keep going as he approached third at full speed . . . and tried to shift into another gear as he headed home.

Cooley's first baseman finally realized what was happening, and he scrambled to recover the ball. He picked it up cleanly, whirled, and threw a wobbly strike toward home.

The crowd gasped, sensing the play at the plate would be close . . . and might be the pivotal moment in the game . . . and maybe the season!

Toby Tyler was chugging toward home as fast as he could, and he could see the ball would beat him there.

But he also saw the throw was going to come up short. The catcher was moving out to get it on the fly, so Toby bore down with all his might trying to force more speed out of his fire-hydrant body.

The ball reached the catcher, who caught it and dove toward home plate and a sliding Toby Tyler. The catcher got there first, and Toby's hard slide carried him right into the glove just in front of the plate.

The umpire's right arm went up, his hand balled in a fist with his thumb sticking skyward . . . and then . . . he saw the ball come trickling out of the catcher's glove and dance away, as Toby Tyler finished his slide across the plate.

"YOU'RE SAFE!!!" shouted the umpire, his hands signaling the safe sign repeatedly.

Hillsdale's players and fans exploded in joy while Josh Lee raced around to third amidst the chaos. Hillsdale 1, Cooley 0.

Cooley was dumbstruck, and the big hometown crowd was stunned . . . the same thing was happening two games in a row! Seth Gardner stood on the mound seething.

He called time, got a new ball, and circled behind the mound to regroup. Gardner took a deep breath, let it out . . . and was out of the inning on one pitch.

Hillsdale was three outs away from staying undefeated.

***

GRANDPA Russell jumped for joy as Toby Tyler hopped up, stomped on home plate for good measure, and gave the Pirates a 1-0 lead.

"You laugh about the rally cap," Grandpa Russell shouted. "But it works every time!"

In the stands, people smiled . . . and hoped . . . *let's get three outs and get out of this rain!*

"Is it me . . . or does that Rally cap always work?" Allison asked Emily.

"Not always," Emily laughed in reply. "But it works often enough for him to keep trying!"

Then, they all stood and cheered as they watched Hulk Thomas stride in from the bullpen area down the left field line toward Coach Wilson, waiting for him at the mound.

"IT'S HULK THOMAS TIME!!!!" Grandpa Russell shouted to the delight of the fans.

"Here you go, Hulk," Coach Wilson said, handing Hulk the ball at the mound. "This is your time . . . shut em' down, and let's go get warm somewhere!"

Hulk just nodded and started his warmups with catcher Bruce Smithers.

Hulk was facing the 8-9-1 hitters and hoped just to blow them away, but with the damp baseballs, he could feel his control was not as fine as he would like.

He started Cooley's number eight-hitter with a pair of four-seamers placed perfectly on the corners. Hulk tried a pair of cutters, which both just missed.

Thinking he could overpower the hitter, Hulk fired a four-seamer on the 2-2 pitch, which was perfectly placed on the hands. The batter made a weak swing and connected off the fists . . . and the ball headed for no man's land down the right field line.

Trip McHenry, Mark Porter, and Gavin Ford all desperately raced toward the bleeder, but the ball fell fair by inches and kicked away from the trio. By the time Trip McHenry got a handle on it and fired it back to the infield, Cooley was set up with a man at second and nobody out!

A shudder went through the Hillsdale side of the bleachers. Grandpa Russell winced, and Emily and Allison both exchanged a glance. *Don't let them score,* they both thought. *We need to win . . . and then go home and dry out.*

Cooley's number nine-hitter stood at the plate and promptly turned to bunt. Hulk Thomas threw it right past him. Strike one.

Pitch number two . . . same result.

Pitch number three . . . the bunt was off . . . the hitter took a mighty swing . . . strike three. One out. Tying run at 2nd base.

The Hillsdale crowd collectively heaved a sigh of relief.

Now Cooley was at the top of their order. The Cougars' leadoff hitter was a pesky lefthander who was a very tough out. He also had a good eye and worked the count to 2-1 when he sprang a surprise of his own . . . and dropped a bunt down the third base line.

Josh Lee was playing fairly deep with a runner at second to prevent a grounder from getting through the infield. He charged hard, barehanded the ball . . . remembered what had just happened to Cooley's third baseman . . . and promptly ate the ball when he looked up to see the speedy Cooley leadoff man was going to be safe at first.

The baserunner at 2nd scampered over to third, giving Cooley runners at the corners and just one out . . . and it lit a fire under their fans.

Hillsdale was officially in trouble . . .

CHAPTER 28
APRIL-SOPHOMORE YEAR

*C*OOLEY'S number two-hitter was next. Hulk Thomas was upset and stalking around behind the mound. Rob Mathews recognized the trouble signs, called time, and trotted over for a chat.

"Come on, Hulk . . . settle down," Rob soothed. "Two cheap hits. You got this . . . you're throwing strikes . . . with great movement . . . and location. Trust your stuff . . . and your defense! Keep doing that, and we're golden!"

Hulk harrumphed . . . and nodded at Rob, setting his jaw tight and standing up on the hill for a sign. He glanced around, seeing the infield was in. Trip McHenry held the runner close at first with a righthanded hitter at the plate. The outfield was drawn in part way, hoping to cut off any cheap hits.

Hulk took a deep breath and let it out slowly as he climbed back onto the mound. He went into the stretch and fired a perfect strike on the outside corner with his cutter. Strike one. Next pitch . . . same spot. Same result. Next pitch . . . a perfect cutter on the hands with movement inside. Swinging strike three. Two outs.

Hillsdale's players breathed a massive sigh of relief . . . and so did the Pirate fans. Two outs. Just one more to stay undefeated in league. The infield and outfield moved back to regular depth. Cooley's number three-hitter strode to the plate, looking to do some damage.

Hulk's confidence is soaring. He looks in at Bruce Smithers behind the plate and grabs the sign. Strike one with a cutter on the inside corner. Ball one . . . a cutter missed on the outside. Ball two . . . a cutter just missed on the outside. Swinging strike two on a four-seamer above the hands . . . was probably ball three. *Thank you, batter,* Hulk thought.

Ball three . . . cutter just inside . . . 3-2 count. *Base to play with,* Hulk thought. *Don't give in. Make a good pitch.*

The rain was starting to come down a little harder, but the umps were determined to get this game over. They looked skyward . . . at each other . . . and the home plate ump waved out to Hulk to make a pitch.

Cutter. Inside corner. Fouled back.

Cutter. Outside corner. Popped up over the first base dugout . . . out of play.

Cutter. On the hands. Topped foul by third base.

Cutter. Low and away. Just got a piece of it.

Cutter. Inside corner. Line drive foul past third base.

Cutter. Left out over the middle. Fouled straight back over the screen. Hitter just missed it. New ball.

Hulk Thomas took the ball and rubbed it up behind the mound. *He's right on the cutter now. Should I throw the four-seamer? No . . . wait . . . the change,* Hulk thought, trying to conceal his grin. *This is the perfect time to throw the changeup . . . he'll never be looking for a change. I'll make him look bad!*

The crowd on both sides of the field were all standing. Pitch number 12 was coming in this epic battle, and both sides wanted a resolution . . . provided it was the happy resolution they wanted.

Both dugouts were on their feet, yelling out encouragement. They both knew the importance of this game . . . it could be the season for Cooley . . . for Hillsdale, a missed chance to stay in control of their own destiny.

Hulk Thomas stood up on the mound and peered at Bruce Smithers. He flashed him the cutter inside and Hulk shook his head no. Smithers flashed the cutter outside . . . the four-seamer . . . no and no. Finally, Bruce Smithers stood up, called time, and shook himself a little bit before walking a few steps out in front of the mound and yelling at Hulk, "Come on, make a decision!"

Smithers settled back in and flashed a cutter inside . . . Smithers really wanted Hulk to throw the cutter inside. Hulk nodded in agreement. *But I'm throwing the change,* Hulk thought stubbornly.

Hulk came set, glanced at both baserunners and went into his motion. The pitch came out of Hulk's hand perfectly and floated toward the plate. Cooley's hitter was fooled . . . and thinking cutter or four-seamer exclusively . . . he was way out in front. As the pitch neared the plate, it fell off the table and dipped below the strike zone. Fortunately, it also dipped below the flailing swing of the batter . . . unfortunately, it dipped right under the glove of a completely fooled catcher who had been expecting a cutter to the inside.

A roar from Hillsdale's fans as strike three was called . . . and then an immediate groan as they saw the ball squirt past Bruce Smithers on the way to the backstop.

Cooley's runner from third was off as the ball kicked free, and he sprinted toward the plate. Bruce Smithers quickly . . . frantically . . . flung off his mask, spotted the ball, and dashed after it, sliding into it and coming up throwing to the plate . . . as Hulk Thomas rumbled in that direction.

As Hulk neared the plate, he saw they had a shot at the runner. The ball was there . . . Hulk reached for it . . . but took his eye off the ball to check the runner. The throw hit Hulk's glove but didn't stick. The ball bounced away up the first base line, the tying run crossed the plate, and Cooley's fans exploded with delight and relief. Hillsdale fans sagged in the dismal, drenched seats.

Hulk recovered enough to spot the ball and raced toward it. He saw the runner from first halfway to third. He pounced on the ball and came up firing . . . just as he heard Rob yelling, "NO THROW, NO THROW!!!"

Too late . . . the wet, slippery ball, now even damper from the grass, slithered out of Hulk's hand crazily . . . and sailed far over Rob's head, who was covering third, and down the left field line into the corner.

Hulk sagged when he saw the ball was a good three feet over Rob's glove . . . and he saw the Cooley runner round third and jog happily home with the winning run.

Cooley and their fans erupted onto the field in a wild celebration.

Hillsdale's fans sat in stunned silence.

The Pirates on the field were staggered.

It was a gut punch.

Hillsdale went from a thrilling 1-0 win to a heartbreaking 2-1 loss in ten seconds.

Rob stood at third base, bewildered. Trip was frozen near first . . . not comprehending what happened. Buck stood in center field . . . his mouth hanging open in disbelief. *What just happened?* the trio thought.

Hulk Thomas stood between home and first in shocked silence . . . feeling anger at himself . . . anger at the Baseball Gods . . . and remorse . . . for being stubborn and stupid! *Why did I throw the change without letting Bruce know? Why did I throw to third when Rob said no throw? Why me? Why did I blow it for the whole team? The whole town? Why?*

CHAPTER 29
APRIL-SOPHOMORE YEAR

GRANDPA Russell, visibly shaken, held the car door open for Emily and quickly opened the back door for Allison Pierce. He lurched around to the driver's side, hauled himself in, and closed the door with a slam.

He shook himself, watched droplets of water spray everywhere, and apologized to the girls.

"Oh, I'm sorry," Grandpa Russell said gruffly.

He started the car and let it idle for a while, letting the heater take over to help warm the threesome up. He sat staring for a long minute, finally letting out a long sigh.

"What in the Sam Hill just happened out there?" Grandpa Russell asked rhetorically. "I've never seen anything like it."

"It's just a game, Dad," Emily started . . . stopping abruptly when he glared at her.

"You know what this game meant . . ." Grandpa Russell began, with fire in his eyes. He turned and glanced at Allison, who had tears in her eyes, and back to Emily . . . who sat staring straight ahead.

"You're right, of course, Em," Grandpa Russell finally said, letting out another long sigh. "It's just that . . . they were so close . . . just so close . . . I'm not sure what happened . . . but I think Hulk crossed Bruce Smithers up."

The girls both looked at Grandpa Russell in bewilderment.

"What do you mean?" Allison asked.

"Looks like Hulk threw him a change-up," Grandpa Russell said. "Something off-speed, anyway... Rob has been working on a change with him, but he wasn't supposed to start throwing it in games until next week. I bet Hulk decided on his own to throw the change... did you notice him shaking Bruce off... and then Bruce going halfway to the mound."

"But, why does it matter?" Allison asked.

"Bruce was probably looking for a fastball or cutter inside," Grandpa Russell lectured. "He sets his body up to receive that pitch... and his mind... then, Hulk throws it down and away... soft... it just crossed him up, and he couldn't get over fast enough to knock it down."

Understanding lit on both Allison and Emily's faces.

"I get it," Allison said. "I bet Hulk feels terrible."

"Yes, no doubt worse than we feel... and that's a lot," Grandpa Russell announced with a deep sigh of resignation.

"Oh, I feel sorry for all of them," Emily chimed in.

"Me, too!" Allison added. *It's like Rob said last year when he gave up that home run in the Sectionals... it's one thing to make a good pitch and get beat... and another to make a bad pitch. I feel awful for Hulk... and for Rob... he takes these things so hard.*

CHAPTER 30
APRIL-SOPHOMORE YEAR

COACH Dave Wilson stood outside the visitor's dugout as his shell-shocked team limped back to the bench. The thought running through his mind was, *what do I say?* He hesitated, thought for a long moment, and followed his last player down the dugout steps.

He took a long look at the most morose group of teenage baseball players he had ever seen and took a deep breath.

"Guys!" Coach Wilson called out sharply, grabbing their attention. "I want you to stand up, get in a line, take five steps forward, and turn around."

The team, confused, rose slowly, assembled into a makeshift line, counted out five steps, and turned around.

Coach Wilson quickly stepped in front of them, now confident his kids did not have to watch Cooley celebrating in short right field.

"Ahem," Coach Wilson cleared his throat. "No way around it, guys . . . this was a tough one!"

The team mumbled and murmured . . . looked down at their feet . . . felt terrible.

"But . . . day's done . . . we can't change what just happened," Coach Wilson continued. "We can only try to control our response and learn from our mistakes. This is a great opportunity . . . a chance to learn and improve!"

Further mumbling and grumbling . . . but an understanding of what Coach Wilson was teaching.

"Let's review the day," Coach Wilson went on. "First, for six innings, you played a tremendous defensive game . . . and Jose . . . you were magnificent on the hill . . . just like you've been all year!"

Finally, something good to respond to . . . and a few positive mumbles emerged.

"You hitters battled a very, very tough pitcher out there . . . hey, we had ten hits and five walks," Coach Wilson said slowly. "But we stranded 14 baserunners."

Groans from the team.

"We got great work from our closer," Coach Wilson continued firmly, "except for one bad pitch . . . just one mental mistake, really . . . and we'll remedy that. Hulk, your stuff was unhittable today . . . two cheap hits and . . ."

Hulk Thomas, his head bowed, looked up to see Coach Wilson staring at him.

"You're still my closer, Hulk," Coach Wilson said sternly. "That's not going to change."

Coach Wilson held Hulk's eyes until Hulk gave him an acknowledging nod and then moved on.

"So, what did we learn today?" Coach Wilson asked.

Hulk Thomas stepped up immediately.

"You don't cross up your catcher," Hulk said with emotion. "I'm sorry, guys . . . it won't happen again."

Hulk bowed his head again, on the verge of tears.

"Hey, no problem," rang out from several players. "We'll get it next time."

"What else?" Coach Wilson asked.

"We've got to stop blowing our scoring chances," Trip McHenry spouted. "I was awful out there today! If I had come through just once, we would have had a big cushion to work with. I apologize, guys."

"Yes, we did miss a lot of chances," Coach Wilson answered. "But how do we solve that?"

"We stop putting so much pressure on ourselves," Rob Mathews said.

"Bingo!" Coach Wilson replied.

"Guys, we preach all week . . . it's the process . . . do your work at practice to get better and then let things take their natural course," Coach Wilson implored. "How many times today . . . in clutch situations . . . did we hit the ball hard? A bunch! They didn't fall in today . . . but they will . . . they will . . . if you keep working hard to be the best you can be. The better you practice, the better you get . . . and the better you are, the more chances you have for that hard-hit ball to fall in."

Coach Wilson paused and scanned the team.

"This one will hurt for a while," Coach Wilson finally said. "But we don't have time to dwell on it. We have Pine Bluff in two days . . . we have to be prepared for that one. Remember, we still control our destiny . . . we win out . . . we are league champs . . . and that's what we're gonna' plan on doing."

Coach Wilson paused again.

"The big thing to remember is this," Coach Wilson said softly, making the kids lean in to hear him. "We control what we can control . . . our attitudes, our work ethic, our baseball smarts, and our process! You do all that, and no matter what happens on the field, you are a success . . . because you're doing your absolute best . . . and that's all we can ask for. But you have to control that . . . do the work . . . take pride in doing it right!"

Coach Wilson let that sink in for a moment.

"Now, get your gear together and get onto the bus . . . be ready for a good practice tomorrow!" Coach Wilson exclaimed, trying to be positive.

The team shuffled off to collect their gear, and Coach Wilson waited a beat and pulled Hulk Thomas outside the dugout.

"Hulk," Coach Wilson began, "we all make mistakes . . ."

"I know, Coach . . . I'm sorry," Hulk answered quickly.

"So, you know what you did wrong?" Coach Wilson asked.

"I threw the change when Bruce called for a cutter," Hulk answered.

"And?" Coach Wilson prompted, but Hulk just looked confused.

"My . . . bad . . . throw," Hulk sputtered.

"Well, that, too . . . did you hear Rob shouting "no throw?" Coach Wilson asked.

"Not . . . until it . . . was . . . too late," Hulk managed.

"The actual throw does not bother me, Hulk," Coach Wilson soothed. "It's the mental part . . . not hearing Rob . . . not listening to Bruce . . . not following my explicit direction that we would not throw the change until next week."

Suddenly, it dawned on Hulk Thomas what his biggest mistake had been.

"Uh, oh . . . yeah . . . I just," Hulk stammered.

"Look, Hulk, being on a team means we all are pulling together . . . all are on the same page," Coach Wilson said. "You were on a different page today . . . the Hulk Thomas page."

Hulk bowed his head and stared at his feet.

"We have a plan for you . . . a good plan . . . for you and the team," Coach Wilson said slowly. "We thought it through, and we're confident it will pay off this year . . . and for the next three years after this one."

Hulk raised his head and looked Coach Wilson in the eye.

"I'll be on the Team page from now on," Hulk said sincerely.

"Yes, you will," Coach Wilson drawled with a smile.

"Look, Hulk . . . you are right there," Coach Wilson added. "Will you be better with that change . . . absolutely . . . was it the right call in that situation . . . probably . . . look how bad you made that hitter look! It shows us how unhittable you will be with the changeup . . . once it's ready."

Hulk nodded, feeling somewhat better.

"But . . . I tell you when we are ready to unveil it . . . and when you throw it . . . so the defense is on the same page," Coach Wilson said sternly. "You know I'm calling those pitches Bruce is putting down signs for, right?"

"Uh, yeah," Hulk answered.

"So, listen to your coach," Coach Wilson said with a small smile.

Hulk just nodded silently.

"You're my closer, Hulk," Coach Wilson said proudly. "You were born to be a closer, and you're mine. Closers have short memories. Forget today . . . get some rest . . . and on Thursday . . . you be ready . . . because you are going to close out Pine Bluff!"

CHAPTER 31

APRIL-SOPHOMORE YEAR

*T*WO hours later, Rob Mathews, Trip McHenry, Buck Buckman, Toby Tyler, Hulk Thomas, and Donnie Fields were huddled around a booth at Pop's Diner in downtown Hillsdale, waiting for their burgers, fries, and shakes.

"I still can't believe we lost to Cooley!" Toby Tyler said for the third time since they had sat down at the booth.

Pop's was busy tonight . . . especially for a Tuesday night in April. The diner was straight out of the 1950s with its booths and counter stools, all adorned with red upholstery on chrome frames. The checkerboard flooring and mini-jukeboxes in the booths completed the "retro" picture.

Tonight, Pop's was filled with people, and the popular eatery was hopping and alive with animated conversation . . . except at the Hillsdale Pirate table.

"We should never have lost that game," Trip piped in. "Cheap win for Cooley . . . but we'll get em' next time."

"Yeah," Donnie Fields spoke up. "That's where you guys are lucky."

Heads popped up, paying attention.

"What do you mean, Donnie?" asked Rob.

"You get another chance at them," Donnie explained. "When I blew the "Pick" game two years ago, I had to wait a whole year to get a chance for redemption . . . and then we lost again!"

The entire table felt Donnie's pain.

Hulk looked up at Donnie when he said that and asked, "Donnie . . . do you ever get over that pain?"

"Yes . . . and no," Donnie said quietly. "I still think about it sometimes . . . but not as often lately . . . you know the old saying . . . time heals everything."

"Yeah, I was afraid of that," Hulk moaned.

"The beauty is . . . you get to go out there Thursday and get back in the saddle . . . it will help you forget today faster," Donnie said.

"Unless I blow it on Thursday, too," Hulk said sulkily.

"You won't," Rob spouted. "Coach said you're his closer . . . he's got confidence in you . . . so do we."

"That's right," came from Toby, Trip, and Buck.

"I know you're hurting, Hulk . . . I blew the Sectionals last year because I had to throw that change . . . I get it," Rob said. "But everybody rallied around me . . . and that helped. We're here for you . . . you . . . and all of us are going to be fine . . . and you're going to shut down Pine Bluff on Thursday."

"Yeah, I'd like to do that," Hulk replied slowly. "Those Danielson boys have been a pain in my neck for a lot of years. Especially Clem . . . but those other two . . . Jeb and Dirk . . . they were always bullying around the sandlot and stuff."

The guy's food arrived, and the topic shifted to high school boy talk . . . girls, driver's licenses, food, the Giants . . . and the Dodgers . . . and their moods lightened.

As their plates were being cleared, there was a commotion at the front door, and the whole table looked over to see Tony Russo and a group of Valley Christian athletes walk into Pop's with a bevy of girls in tow.

Trip stiffened as he saw them heading their way . . . and he noticed his old girlfriend Jenny and her friend Lacy were part of the group.

"Well, well, well, look at the loser table over there," Tony crowed loudly, walking toward where the Hillsdale guys sat.

"Look, everybody . . . it's the "Candy Boys," Tony laughed.

The table looked back at him in confusion.

"Oh, sorry . . . you go to public school . . . you're a little dense," Tony smirked. "I'll take it slow for you . . . the "M&M Boys" . . . from the newspaper . . . M&M's are candy."

The Valley Christian group howled, and Trip noticed Jenny and Lacy were laughing, too.

"What do you want, Russo?" Trip snapped.

"Nothing much . . . just wanted to congratulate you on your plan," Tony said with a smirk.

"Plan?" Trip asked warily.

"Yeah . . . your plan to keep your promise of never losing to Valley Christian again in Basketball or Baseball," Tony laughed.

The Hillsdale guys looked perplexed.

"I'll explain it slowly again . . . so you'll understand it," Tony said. "You plan to lose to nobodies like Cooley . . . so that you don't make the playoffs . . . and you can't play us. We don't play . . . you don't lose. Pretty smart plan for a bunch of losers."

Trip could feel his face get red and his temper building.

"Of course, your master stroke in the plan was to make old Tubby Thomas here, your closer. You'll never make the playoffs with Tubby in that role," Tony laughed cruelly.

Hulk Thomas tensed and glanced at Trip, thinking the pair could do some damage in a fight with these guys.

"Real funny, Tony," Rob interjected. "Now, why don't you take your sideshow somewhere else."

Rob looked at the other Hillsdale guys and exuded calm.

"Yeah . . . our booth is ready anyway," Tony responded. "Don't want to be seen hanging out with you losers for too long . . . it might be catching . . . or wait . . . not for us . . . we're Valley Christian . . . not Hillsdale."

Trip and Hulk both started to stand . . . and Rob bolted upright in a hurry and gestured for them to sit down. Tony and his group backed off.

"Yeah, well, catch you later, losers," Tony said as they walked away. "Much later, because we won't be seeing you in the baseball sectionals . . . but you can't run away from it, McHenry . . . we'll see you next fall in our Thanksgiving Basketball Tourney. That's when we'll be able to shut you up for good . . . Hillsdale beating VC . . . what a joke."

"Well, that was pleasant," Buck announced as the Valley Christian mob moved away.

"I wish we played them in football," Toby Tyler proclaimed.

"We'll get them this baseball season," Trip said defiantly. "And we'll beat em'!"

"You got that right!!!" Hulk Thomas said with a sneer. "I have taken as much as I am going to take from that guy!"

Rob listened intently . . . saw the fire in the guy's eyes . . . and he smiled. *We're going all the way this season!*

CHAPTER 32
APRIL-SOPHOMORE YEAR

*T*HE mood at Hillsdale High was fairly upbeat on Wednesday ... after all ... baseball was not like football ... or even basketball for that matter. Baseball did not inspire schoolwide or citywide concern like the other two sports.

Still, there were the baseball players who were somber ... but determined ... and their friends knew enough not to cross any lines with the team after yesterday's loss to Cooley.

After lunch, in science class, Allison Pierce and Lisa Cruz sat huddled together during lab time ... doing their experiment and ... talking about Rob Mathews.

"So, you have convinced me," Lisa whispered, looking to see if anyone was listening.

"About ... ?" Allison prompted.

"Rob," Lisa replied. "I'm going to ask him to Prom ... and Jillian says she is going ask Trip ... and maybe we'll double!"

"Oh, Lisa ... that's great," Allison replied sincerely. *Why do I do this to myself?* she thought as she smiled at Lisa.

"I'm kind of excited about it," Lisa continued. "Having another couple will help just in case ... and Rob has been so friendly lately ... and he's just so funny."

I know, I know, I love him! Allison screamed internally.

"He's a great guy, Lisa," Allison said instead. "You guys will make a great couple."

"Well, I don't know if it will go anywhere," Lisa giggled. "What will he be like out of class ... you know ... to talk to him alone ... maybe dance ... and stuff ... you know."

Oh, Lisa, you may be in for a shock, Allison thought, thinking of Rob and Stephanie Miller.

"Oh, you'll be fine," Allison responded. "Rob's not the biggest on dancing ... he prefers the slow ones ... but you never know."

"Well, I'm excited to see how we do ... he's such a stud ... I can't wait to slow dance with him!" Lisa gushed.

Allison started to roll her eyes but caught herself in time and smiled at Lisa instead.

"I'm going to ask him today," Lisa said excitedly. "Are you sure he'll say yes?"

Allison paused, looked over at Rob, and back at Lisa.

"I think I'd wait on asking him," Allison whispered. "He's not in the best mood after yesterday's game ... he might just say no because he's kinda' bummed."

Lisa stopped abruptly and faced Allison.

"Yeah ... you're right," Lisa said knowingly. "I get that. The question is, what if they lose to Pine Bluff tomorrow ... he might not ever say yes if that happens!"

The girls giggled some more.

A year ago, I would have never understood that mentality, Allison thought. *But Lisa gets it ... she's an athlete, too. She gets it ... I think I do, too ... now.*

"Yeah, I think I'll wait until Friday if they win ... next week if they don't," Lisa said finally.

"Good idea," Allison answered while thinking, *I wonder if I can somehow stop this now? Lisa is perfect for Rob. What have I done?*

CHAPTER 33

APRIL-SOPHOMORE YEAR

HULK Thomas stood on Rob's mound at the "APF" and rubbed up the baseball. After a good practice with the team at school, Rob, Trip, and Hulk adjourned to the "APF" for a little work on Hulk's change-up.

The session had gone remarkably well, as Hulk's feel for the pitch was improving daily, and it was obvious to Rob that it was close to being game-ready. *Coach Wilson will be excited,* Rob thought.

Hulk stared down at Rob for the target, rocked, and threw a perfect change that danced at the edge of the outside corner at the knees and then fell off the table as it reached the plate.

"Awesome pitch, Hulk!" Trip and Rob said at the same time.

Hulk smiled and readied himself for another pitch.

Boom. Same pitch. Perfect spot.

"You are looking great, Hulk," Rob enthused. "Let's do five more, and we're done until next week!"

Hulk got the ball back and climbed onto the mound. Looking to his left, he noticed Allison Pierce approaching, and he smiled shyly and waved his glove at her. Allison smiled, waved back, stopped behind him close to the street, and watched as the lesson continued.

Five near-perfect changeups later, Hulk was lumbering off the mound toward Trip and Rob and into a group hug between home plate and the pitcher's mound.

"That was great, Hulk," Rob said excitedly. "Next week we unveil it . . . and the sky's the limit! I think it is going to be so effective . . . I can't wait to see it in action!"

"You sure we can't use it tomorrow?" Hulk asked.

"Yeah, Coach wants to wait until next week . . . then you can break it in . . . get used to throwing it in games before the Sectionals!" Rob said confidently. "Besides, you can close out Pine Bluff with your cutter!"

Allison smiled as she watched Rob work with Hulk. *He really knows how to instill confidence in a kid!*

"Hey, Ally, what's happening?" Trip asked loudly, noticing her for the first time.

"Just watching my heroes . . . in person . . . up close and personal!" Allison replied sarcastically.

"Well, enjoy it now," Trip drawled in response. "Tomorrow, you won't be able to get close to us after we beat Pine Bluff!"

As the four laughed, a car squealed around the corner and sped past them, with their car stereo blaring rap music. Suddenly, the car screeched to a halt . . . hesitated . . . and then backed slowly toward them.

Rob groaned audibly when he saw who it was . . . Jeb, Dirk, and Clem Danielson . . . along with Jake "The Snake" Gardner.

"Well, lookie here," Jeb said, curling his hands tightly around the steering wheel. "The three biggest losers from Hillsdale High."

Rob, Trip, and Hulk were trying to ignore the guys from Pine Bluff and turned to move toward the house, with Rob motioning Allison to come with them.

"Hey, what's the matter, losers . . . don't want to talk with your friends?" Jeb asked snidely.

"What are you doing around here, Jeb?" Rob asked, turning and stopping.

"Oh, old Jake here told us you lived around here . . . we thought we'd come over and ask you . . . just how exactly you lost to Cooley???!!! Hah! What a bunch of losers!!!" Jeb cackled.

No response.

"What did they expect," Clem Danielson spoke up for the first time. "How could they win using Tubby Thomas as their closer!!???"

Hulk Thomas froze.

"Don't call me that, Clem!" Hulk growled.

"Why not, Tubby . . . we've been calling you that since the third grade!" Clem sneered. "And, the third grade might be the last time you got me out in a baseball game . . . and you ain't ever got brother Jeb out!"

"That'll change tomorrow," Hulk growled again.

The foursome burst out laughing hard.

"You guys need to have a lead to use a closer . . ." Jeb laughed. "That ain't happening. Get used to it . . . your season's over tomorrow, losers."

"Time for you guys to leave," Trip McHenry announced gruffly, moving toward the car.

"Oh, we're real scared," Jake Gardner spouted from the safety of the back seat.

"You did what you came for . . . now get out of here before you get hurt," Trip snarled.

Jeb Danielson's hands gripped the steering wheel harder, calculating the situation. *We got four to their three . . . but McHenry and Thomas are huge . . . and Mathews can take care of himself . . . we can beat em', but it might get ugly.*

"Besides," Jeb said, suddenly calm and amiable. "We haven't finished what we came for."

"What's that?" Trip asked.

"We heard you were really generous with your old girlfriends, McHenry . . . passing them around to guys at other schools . . . and Jake here says Hillsdale girls are the best looking around here . . . so we thought we'd come find us some for ourselves!"

Silence.

Jeb looked around . . . noticed Allison for the first time and laughed out loud, pointing at Allison and staring at her in disbelief.

"Jake . . . what are you talking about . . . look at the geek over there," Jeb howled. "This is definitely not the neighborhood to find hot girls . . . she is awful!"

"That's enough, Jeb!" Rob roared, advancing toward the car in a hurry.

Allison was frozen, shocked at how the conversation had shifted to her.

"We know that's your girlfriend, Mathews . . . Jake told us," Clem sneered.

"What a dog," Jeb roared, looking straight at Allison.

Allison burst into tears, turned, and ran home, slamming the front door behind her.

"You jerk," Rob cried out, reaching the car door and grabbing Jeb by the shoulder, trying to pull him out of the car.

Rob was in an angry frenzy and clawed at the door handle before Trip grabbed his arms and pulled him away.

"Get out of here now!!!" Trip yelled. "Or, get out of the car, and let's do this!!!"

Jeb collected himself and sat up straight behind the wheel.

"Losers," he called out, and as Trip started closing the gap between himself and the car door, Jeb slammed the car in gear and peeled out.

"What the heck was that?" Trip said, exhaling as Jeb's car skittered around the car and out of sight. He glanced at Rob, watching closely as Rob tried to simmer down. *Wow, Rob got intense there. Never seen him like that before.*

"Those guys are just jerks . . . always have been . . . just like Tony Russo . . . always been jerks," Hulk said.

"You've known them since you were little?" Trip asked.

"I've never been little, Trip," Hulk said with a soft laugh. "Tubby . . . I earned that name . . . probably still do," Hulk said, patting his still-soft stomach. "But I'm going to show em' tomorrow . . . they're going to have to start calling me something else . . . Closer."

"I like it," Trip smiled. "How about you, Rob?"

Trip turned and saw Rob moving toward Allison's house.

"How about you?" Trip asked again.

"Love it!" Rob called back.

"Where you going?" Trip asked.

"To see Allison," Rob answered.

"I like it," Trip said under his breath. "I like it."

CHAPTER 34
APRIL-SOPHOMORE YEAR

"*A*LLISON, it's OK," Rob said as Allison lay on her bed crying hard. *What in the heck should I do? What am I doing here? In Allison's bedroom . . . when she's crying!*

Rob stepped closer to the bed.

"Ally . . . Ally," Rob said softly.

Allison gulped and tried to stop her tears . . . but she only managed to slow them down as she turned her tear-stained face to his.

"Ally," Rob said, looking directly in her eyes. "You can't listen to those guys . . . they don't know what they're talking about!"

Oh, man, when she takes her glasses off, Allison's eyes are really beautiful, Rob noticed again. *They just sparkle . . . even through all the tears.*

Allison continued crying.

"Those guys are just jerks . . . you've heard them at our games . . . you just have to tune them out," Rob said soothingly.

"Yeah . . . easy for you to say . . . but . . . you're . . . not . . . an . . . ugly . . . girl," Allison whimpered.

"Allison . . . you're not ugly," Rob managed.

"Well, I'm sure not beautiful," Allison said, trying to laugh but failing miserably.

"You're beautiful inside, Ally," Rob squeaked out.

What???!!! Did I really just say that? Rob thought in horror. *What is wrong with me? I have been hanging around girls too much... Mom... Allison...*

"Rea... really," Allison sputtered. *Did he really just say that? And he called me Ally! I love it when he calls me Ally!*

"Really," Rob stated.

Allison sat up and dabbed at her tears.

"Why... why... were they so mean... mean... to me?" Allison asked wearily. "I didn't do anything to them..."

"Because they are just mean, period," Rob answered honestly. "There is something inside them... I can't explain it... but I know it's there. They just like making people feel bad ... small... I don't know..."

Allison nodded, gave a little sob, caught it, and forced it down.

"That's all they know how to do... it's kinda' sad," Rob added.

Allison nodded again, still fighting the urge to cry.

"What can I do for you, Ally?" Rob asked. "You are always there for me... I want to be there for you... you're... you're my best friend. Let me know what I can do to help you ... anything..."

Allison sobbed again... this time a sob of happiness.

"Could... you... could you just... hold... hold... me for a second?" Allison finally managed, gazing at Rob hopefully.

Rob froze. *Hold her... oh geez... hold her?*

She looked up at him and tried to give him her special smile, but it was half-hearted at best. Rob tried to return the smile, but his was forced, too.

Rob reached down, took her hands, and pulled her up from the bed. His arms went around her, and she relaxed and nestled close to him.

They stood still . . . silent . . . for two minutes . . . two long minutes . . . both of them trying to figure out what they were feeling . . . and Rob initially thinking, *how can I end this?* After a moment, he had second thoughts . . . *wait . . . this . . . Allison . . . feels pretty good in my arms! What is this feeling???*

Allison's mind was racing . . . mainly with joy. *What those jerks said really hurts . . . but this . . . this is wonderful. I could stay like this forever.*

Rob was clueless. *What the heck is happening? But . . . it feels nice . . . it feels natural. In ways . . . I don't want this to end. No . . . no way! Me and Allison? No way!!! Still . . .*

CHAPTER 35
APRIL-SOPHOMORE YEAR

*R*OB continued warming up his arm in the right field bullpen at Hillsdale's Baseball/Softball complex . . . Jeb Danielson was doing the same for the Pine Bluff Warriors in left field.

Here we go again, Rob thought, as he got a feel for each pitch he would need today to beat the Warriors. *It just seems like every time I look up we're playing Pine Bluff in a critical game . . . and this one is huge!*

Rob scanned the already massive crowd and spotted his Mom in her customary spot behind the hometown dugout. Grandpa Russell was there . . . and Grandma Russell, too . . . along with Trip's Aunt Barb and her boys. The weather had warmed up . . . and it was a picture-perfect late April day in the California foothills.

But where's Allison? Rob pondered, not seeing her in her usual spot. *She was a little weird this morning . . . after yesterday, who wouldn't be? I was weird, too. I hope yesterday doesn't change anything . . .*

They had walked together to school, but their usual banter was stilted and subdued. Neither one was sure what to make of their prolonged hug yesterday evening. During the day, they exchanged looks across the classroom or the corridor . . . but they didn't speak at all . . . and Allison had not flashed her signature smile.

Focus, Rob thought, as his warmup time was winding down. *Can't be thinking about Allison now. Still . . . where is she? She needs to be here to see this game . . . to help me be confident. Wait! What? Help me be confident? What is wrong with me? Why do I need Allison here to be confident? What?*

Knowing she did not want to be late today, Allison Pierce was hustling down the street toward the park at that moment . . . thinking about yesterday . . . and Rob.

What did yesterday really mean? Allison wondered for the 100th time since last night. *He called me beautiful inside . . . didn't argue that I was a dog . . . but that's just Rob's way. I know I'm ugly . . . but Rob at least thinks I'm beautiful inside. Will he ask me out? No, no way . . . he only dates hot girls . . . you've heard him talk about girls. Remember, wait until he's older . . . and more mature.*

Allison rounded the corner, showed her Student ID at the gate, and clamored for the bleachers just as Rob started heading toward the dugout for the final team meeting before game time.

Rob looked up as he started going down the dugout steps, and there she was. They both stopped . . . stared . . . frozen . . .

Allison took a deep breath, and there it was . . . her best smile, braces and all. Rob hesitated . . . but just for a second . . . and returned her smile, suddenly feeling warm all over. *How does she do that to me?* Rob wondered.

"Good luck, Rob," she called out gaily.

"Thanks, Ally" Rob replied, ducking into the dugout.

Ally! I love it when he calls me Ally! Allison rejoiced, before flashing another big smile and working her way to her seat between Emily and Grandpa Russell.

Good! Now I'm ready, Rob thought as he gathered with his team and Coach Wilson. *Now, focus on baseball . . . and on beating Pine Bluff!*

***

"**Y**OU guys all know how important this game is," Coach Wilson began. "I heard about the little run-in at the "APF" yesterday . . . and we can use that . . . but only if we're smart about it. Does it give us extra motivation? Sure it does . . . but we can't let that . . . or how big the game is . . . get in the way of how we go about our business today. We play our game . . . our game!"

The team mumbled in agreement.

"Remember, our goal is always to play the best we can, regardless of who we're playing," Coach Wilson continued. "That's why you've probably noticed I'm more upset after a blowout win . . . if we didn't play our best . . . didn't focus our best . . . then I am if you lose a tough, well-played game. It's all about doing our best . . ."

The team smiled in acknowledgment . . . they knew that was true.

"Our mantra all year has been . . . focus . . . relax . . . fundamentals," Coach Wilson added. "Play this game doing that . . . and what will be . . . will be. But make sure you stay focused and do the fundamentals we have worked on all year. And . . . do stay relaxed . . . take pride in what you do on every single pitch . . . every play . . . every swing . . . but the more relaxed you are, the better. Don't let anger at Pine Bluff get in the way."

Coach Wilson paused and looked over his team.

"Determination? Absolutely. Motivated to make them pay for yesterday? Absolutely. But make them pay by focusing . . . relaxing . . . and sending them home losers!" Coach Wilson finished.

CHAPTER 36
APRIL-SOPHOMORE YEAR

ROB led his team onto the field and made the short jog to the pitcher's mound for the top of the 1st inning. After his last warm-up toss, the ball flew down to second and went around the horn, with the infield collapsing toward Rob.

Toby Tyler was at third, with Josh Lee moving to short since Rob was pitching. Toby got the last toss and underhanded the ball to Rob.

"Let's do this," Toby chirped, and the infield ran back to get into position . . . except Trip McHenry . . . who moved closer to Rob.

"Yeah . . . let's do this . . . you and me," Trip said quietly. "Let's do this for Hulk."

"Yeah," Rob confirmed. "Let's do it for Hulk . . . and for Allison . . ."

Trip, who had turned to first base, stopped on a dime.

"Hulk can do it for himself," Trip said with determination. "This one's for Allison!"

Rob nodded, and Trip scampered to first base. Rob scanned the stands and found Allison . . . sitting with his Mom and Grandparents. He caught her eye, and they locked in . . . and he slowly tipped his cap to her and turned to face home plate.

***

*T*HE afternoon sun was warm, and Rob felt loose and relaxed. He started the game with a changeup . . . and Pine Bluff's leadoff hitter was completely fooled . . . was way out in front and lofted a lazy pop fly to Trip at first. Out number one.

Batter two took two pitches . . . one a strike and one a ball, before hitting a routine grounder to short. Out number two.

Now came the Danielson boys, hitting 3-4-5 in the order. First came Jeb, followed by Dirk, and then Clem.

Jeb stood at the plate and glared out at Rob with pure hatred. He took his time settling in the box, holding his right hand up for the umpire to see he wasn't ready yet.

Finally, Jeb lowered his hand and put his full attention on Rob.

Rob let him wait. He studied Bruce Smithers for a sign for a long moment. And then he nodded . . . but stood there some more.

Jeb was getting anxious . . . he was antsy to hit. He finally called time, backed out, and climbed back in, ready to hit.

Rob let him wait some more . . . but as Jeb was thinking about stepping out again, Rob started his windup.

Rob started Jeb off with a slow, dancing curve, which hugged the outside corner for a called strike one.

Rob stayed deliberate, sensing how anxious Jeb was to do something big . . . right now.

The change was next, and Jeb flailed at it weakly. Strike two.

Rob looked in for another sign, taking his time . . . milking Jeb Danielson . . . got the sign he wanted and started his wind up.

Jeb was ready to pounce on the fastball he knew was coming.

Change up. Down and away. Weak swing. Strike three.

Time to hit.

Rob trotted toward the dugout, heard Jeb growl something under his breath, and continued on his way. As he got close, he glanced into the stands and saw Allison staring at him, mouthing the words, "Thank you!"

He smiled at her and tipped his cap.

***

As the offense got ready to hit in the bottom of the 1st, Trip McHenry pulled them together.

"Guys . . . we are doing this today," Trip began. "We are beating that smug jerk out there . . . and we're doing it right away."

But . . . it didn't quite work out that way. Buck Buckman and Rob Mathews had singles in the first . . . but Trip and Bruce Smithers could not produce that big hit.

After Rob sailed through the top of the 2nd with three strikeouts, the Pirates got another couple of baserunners in the bottom half before Buck Buckman lined out to end the inning.

The frustration started to mount.

"We've got to stop missing these chances," Grandpa Russell moaned after Buck's line drive was caught in center.

Allison and Emily nodded at his wisdom and tried to think only positive thoughts . . . but that was getting difficult to do for Hillsdale fans . . . not hitting in the clutch was getting really old . . .

CHAPTER 37

APRIL-SOPHOMORE YEAR

***B**ACK* on the mound, Rob was perfect again in the third, with a couple of routine grounders and a great running catch by Buck in the right-center gap.

With one out in the 3rd, Rob missed a homer by inches, winding up at 2nd base, with a stand-up double. Trip McHenry drew a walk . . . but Bruce Smithers and Toby Tyler couldn't get the job done, and it remained scoreless.

In the 4th, Rob finally allowed a baserunner on a one-out flare that fell just in front of Gavin Ford in right. One pitch later, the inning was over . . . when Jeb Danielson rapped into a double play . . . Josh Lee to Mark Porter to Trip McHenry.

Jeb came unglued at the call and had to be held back by his first base coach to keep from being tossed from the game by the umpire.

Danielson was settled down by the time he reached the mound and bullied his way to a perfect bottom of the 4th. The big crowd began to sense they might be in for another classic pitcher's duel.

Rob did his part in the top of the 5th, allowing just a two-out walk, along with a fly ball and a pair of strikeouts.

The crowd was getting restless, and so was Coach Wilson. *We need to score . . . this not hitting in the clutch is killing us,* he thought.

"Hulk . . . start to get stretched out. I want you ready to close once we get a lead," Coach Wilson said confidently, so the whole team could hear him as they got ready to hit in the bottom of the 5th inning.

Buck Buckman was leading off, and the Hillsdale side of the field started buzzing as he made his way to the plate.

Jeb Danielson stared him down . . . he knew Buck well . . . knew just how dangerous he was . . . and knew he had to be careful.

Jeb just missed the corners on several pitches, trying to be too fine, and Buck wisely and patiently worked him for a walk.

The crowd buzzed louder.

Buck danced away from first, trying to draw Jeb's attention, causing Jeb to throw over several times to keep him close. Finally, he came to the plate. Mark Porter turned around to bunt . . . and the pitch was coming straight at him. He tried to get out of the way, but it plunked him in the side.

Porter went down in a heap, and Coach Wilson rushed out to assess the damage. With the wind knocked out of him, Mark Porter took a minute to recover and then trotted down to first, with Buck moving to second.

During the break, Rob and Trip stood together in the on-deck circle, glaring out at Jeb Danielson . . . who gladly returned the favor.

"The dude is cocky," Trip said to Rob. "Gotta' give him credit, though . . . a lot of guys would fall apart."

"Not Jeb," Rob answered flatly.

Rob glanced up in the stands. Hillsdale's fans were all on their feet in anticipation.

"This is our time," spouted Grandpa Russell. "Everybody, it's . . . Rally Cap time!!!"

Allison gave Emily a look . . . and she wrinkled her nose in joy.

"That's my Dad," Emily said, half proud and half embarrassed.

How many times has he said that this year? Allison recalled. *And how many times did it not work?*

Allison saw Rob look her way . . . and he nodded to her with a slight smile.

He's going to do it, Allison thought instantly.

Now it was time. Bottom of the 5th in a scoreless game. A must-win for Hillsdale . . . if they lose, they drop two games behind in the standings at the halfway mark. Serious hole. Pine Bluff loses . . . it's a three-way tie for first.

Rob looked at Trip as the umpire motioned for play to resume.

"This is our time," Rob said to Trip. "For Allison!"

"For Allison!" Trip echoed.

Rob turned and strode to the plate, glaring at Jeb the whole way. Jeb, stone-faced, never looked away.

Rob approached the plate and cleared his head. *Now is just about hitting,* Rob thought. *See the ball . . . hit the ball. React to the pitch. Smooth swing. Head down. Hit it hard somewhere.*

Rob settled in and stared out at Jeb with determination. *This is for you, Ally,* he thought.

First pitch. Cutter. Out over the plate. A mistake.

Boom. A bullet. Right up the middle.

Jeb's eyes get big. The ball screaming right at him. He flings his glove up to protect his face . . .

The ball hits the leather on his closed glove and bounces crazily into the hole between third and short. Buck and Mark are frozen at first . . . the ball was hit so hard . . . everything was happening so fast.

Once it was apparent the ball would hit the ground, both runners exploded to make it safely to the next base. Thinking the ball was going into center field, Rob got a late start but roared down the line toward first.

Clem Danielson scurried after the ball and corralled it just in time to keep Buck Buckman from dashing to the plate.

When the dust settled, Jeb Danielson rose from the seat of his pants and smiled. *Nobody scored. These guys can't hit in the clutch. We'll get out of this,* he thought.

Jeb got the baseball, rubbed it up, and collected himself . . . while the rest of his team followed suit.

Bases loaded, and nobody out. Trip McHenry, Bruce Smithers, and Toby Tyler coming up.

Now, all the fans in the entire stadium were on their feet . . . screaming encouragement to their teams.

Trip McHenry made his way to the batter's box. He turned slightly as he approached, glanced back to the stands, and saw Allison. He stopped and stared her way . . . caught her eye . . . and smiled . . . and nodded her way.

Allison saw the look and took a deep breath. *Don't do this for me . . . do it for the team! But no matter what . . . just do it!*

CHAPTER 38
APRIL-SOPHOMORE YEAR

TRIP stepped into the box and stared out at Jeb Danielson. *I never liked this guy,* Trip thought. *Now, I like him less than ever. He is going down . . . right now. This one's for you, Allison!*

Jeb Danielson toed the rubber and glared in for a sign. *I'll get this guy,* Jeb thought . . . *here comes the change, sucker!*

Just see the ball . . . hit the ball, Trip thought. *Expect the fastball . . . react to the slow stuff.*

Jeb came set and threw what he thought was the perfect pitch . . . down and away . . . dropping out of the zone.

Trip saw the pitch . . . recognized change away . . . shifted his weight . . . stayed back . . . stepped into the pitch . . . and rifled a loud shot directly at shortstop Clem Danielson.

The baserunners froze . . . Clem leaped, stretching his glove out as far as possible.

Over his glove . . . on the way to the left-center field fence!

Buck walks home, Mark Porter ambles homes, and Rob Mathews puts on the afterburners streaking around the bases. Coach Wilson waves him home . . . a very close play at the plate . . . high throw . . . smooth pop-up slide. Rob on his feet, hands held high in the air in triumph . . . looking toward second, where Trip McHenry is pumping his fist and pointing to home plate . . . then to the dugout . . . to Allison Pierce . . . and at Jeb Danielson.

Hillsdale 3, Pine Bluff 0!

Two more innings to go. Six more outs. Never celebrate too early.

***

ROB basked in the glow of the clutch hitting for all of two minutes.

Somehow, Jeb Danielson collected himself again . . . and got out of the 5th without allowing any more runs. Bruce Smithers hit the ball hard . . . but right at the second baseman for an out. Toby Tyler followed with a rocket to short . . . and Clem Danielson made a phenomenal stop, held Trip at 2nd, and threw Tyler out at first. Matt Bryant followed with a strikeout, and the inning was over just like that.

It was up to Rob and the defense to get the game to Hulk Thomas time.

They were up to the task.

Rob got the first hitter on a strikeout. The next hitter bounced a clean single to center, and Hulk Thomas got up and headed down to the bullpen to be safe. He needn't have bothered.

Pine Bluff's lineup turned over, and their leadoff hitter came up and drove a smash between first and second . . . but Trip McHenry dove headlong long, snow-coned the catch in the web of his glove, bounced up, and fed Rob covering first just in time for the second out.

With two outs and a runner at second, the number two-hitter smoked one to left-center . . . but Buck Buckman glided over and made a difficult running catch look easy . . . sending the game to the bottom of the 6th . . . but very quickly that became the top of 7th, as Jeb Danielson made quick work of the bottom three of the Hillsdale order.

Now . . . it was Hulk Thomas time . . . and all he had to do was get three outs to put Hillsdale back in first. The first three hitters . . . Jeb Danielson . . . Dirk Danielson . . . Clem Danielson.

***

H*ULK* picked up the ball behind the mound and thought back to all the times he had been in this position against the Danielson boys. *Not too many good memories,* he thought. *This day . . . this day is going to be a good one!*

"Oh my," Grandpa Russell fretted. "I hope Coach is not making a mistake taking Rob out . . . and putting Hulk in!"

That thought was coursing through the Hillsdale side of the bleachers, and there was unease throughout the stands.

But . . . as the inning began, every Hillsdale fan and player was on their feet shouting out encouragement to Hulk Thomas and the defense.

The Danielson boys stood together in front of their dugout, getting ready to hit. They were all watching Hulk Thomas . . . and would laugh at him any time Hulk would look their way.

As Hulk threw his last warmup pitch, Jeb Danielson walked toward the plate and, in a loud whisper, said, "Looks like our time now, Tubby. You ain't ever got us out . . . it sure ain't gonna' start today."

Hulk glared at him. Jeb laughed heartily.

Strike one. Jeb stopped laughing.

Strike two. Jeb tightened his jaw.

Swinging strike three. Jeb stomped off, back to the dugout, throwing his bat against the fence.

One down.

The crowd roared its approval.

Dirk is next. Three pitches. Three cutters. Ball never touches bat.

Two down.

The crowd is beside itself and are all roaring Hulk's name . . . chanting it as loud as they can. "HULK . . . HULK . . . HULK!!!"

Hulk stands tall and looks around his infield. Sees Rob smiling and nodding. Sees Trip do the same. Feels strong. Feels dominant. Feels unhittable.

And, now . . . it's Clem Danielson.

Cutter. On the hands. Swing through. Strike one.

Crowd noise is unbelievable . . . especially for a baseball game!

Cutter. Movement comes back to nip the outside corner. Called strike two.

Hulk gets the ball. Stares in at the plate. *Clem looks confused,* Hulk thinks. *He's never seen the cutter from me. Maybe I should throw the change? Yes! . . . No! Get the sign and do what you're told.*

Hulk stares in at Bruce Smithers. *Cutter up an in. Yes, sir, Coach Wilson.*

Cutter. Up and in. Weak swing. Strike out the side on nine pitches . . . with no contact.

Bedlam!

Three-way tie for first!

CHAPTER 39
APRIL-SOPHOMORE YEAR

HULK Thomas was in heaven. The crowd erupted and mobbed the field . . . and Hulk . . . but not before his entire team did it first.

And then . . . then . . . he got to stand up and stare at the three Danielson thugs . . . the guys who had tormented him for years . . . and watch them in misery as the Pirates celebrated.

As the celebration waned, Hulk moved through the crowd, close to the Pine Bluff dugout, where the Danielson brothers huddled together in disbelief.

"Hey, guys," Hulk said to them with a wide grin. "Better get used to what you saw today . . . and you can call me Tubby all you want from now on . . . because I can always remind you how Tubby took you down today . . . it will always feel good to hear that name from now on! Enjoy your night . . . I know I'm going to enjoy mine!"

***

ROB and Trip intended to enjoy their night, and they did just that. They got the OK from Rob's Mom and Trip's Aunt Barb while still at the field and headed downtown with most of the team.

Coach Wilson was nearby during their brief conversation and smiled up at Emily, still in the stands, as Rob and Trip hurried off.

"That was quite a nice win today, Dave," Emily said, just a little bit shyly.

"Thanks, Emily," he smiled at her again. "We needed it. It was nice to see us bounce back after Tuesday . . . and get the big hit . . . finally!"

"Yes, that was great . . . and about time, too!" Grandpa Russell butted in as he and Grandma Russell made their way carefully down the bleachers, followed by Allison Pierce.

"Yes, it was about time, Mr. Russell," Coach Wilson laughed. "Your grandson almost took Jeb's head off. What a rip!"

"Yes, yes, he's quite something . . . but Trip . . . he came through with the big one," Grandpa Russell added.

"Yes, sir, he did," Coach Wilson replied.

Grandma and Grandpa Russell reached solid ground and turned to go . . . but Grandpa Russell stopped short.

"Enough of that, sir, and Mr. Russell stuff, Coach," Grandpa Russell said. "I'm Keith, and this is Florence."

"Yes, sir . . . uh, OK, Keith, thanks," Coach Wilson stumbled.

"You coming, Em?" Grandpa Russell asked.

"No, no . . . I think I'll walk home . . . it's such a nice evening," Emily said. "Allison . . . do you want to walk home together?"

"Uh, sure . . . maybe," Allison answered. "Are Rob and Trip still in the dugout, Coach?"

"No, they took off downtown for pizza . . . with the team," Coach Wilson replied. "In fact, I've got to get this place cleaned up . . . they want me to join them."

Emily and Allison both were disappointed . . . the guys were going to be busy tonight.

"Well, congratulations again, Dave," Emily said, turning to go.

"Emily," Coach Wilson said, causing her to stop and turn to face him. "Uh, thanks, Emily," he managed. "Appreciate it. See you soon."

Emily turned to go, and Allison called out.

"Wait up, Emily . . . still want me to walk home with you?" Allison asked.

"Sure," Emily said as they walked toward the street.

"Disappointed Rob and Trip were gone?" Emily asked.

"Yes," Allison replied. "You, uh . . . uh . . . heard about yesterday, I guess?" Allison asked.

"Yes, yes," Emily answered with a warm smile.

"I got your Mom's version first . . . and a shorter version from Rob," Emily laughed.

"It was so sweet of him . . . of Trip and Hulk, too," Allison said softly. "But, especially Rob . . . when he came to my house and . . . and hugged me and stuff."

"I'm not sure he realizes what he did," Emily laughed again. "He is so clueless."

"Well, and then this afternoon . . . at the game . . . he and Trip both kept looking at me and smiling and nodding," Allison said, clearly perplexed.

"I saw that, too," Emily said. "I think they were trying to tell you they were playing this game for you . . . you know . . . dedicating it to you . . . they felt bad how that went yesterday."

Allison's eyes brimmed with tears.

"But, sweetie," Emily said softly. "Don't go getting your hopes up about Rob . . . it's still too early . . . he still . . . he still has to mature a little . . . maybe a lot . . . figure out what's important and what's not . . . it may still take him a while . . ."

Emily paused and turned to give Allison a quick hug.

"It might take years," Emily laughed hard, and Allison joined in while she dried her eyes.

CHAPTER 40
APRIL-SOPHOMORE YEAR

*S*CHOOL was buzzing on Friday morning, with the tale of Hulk Thomas taking out the Danielson boys on nine pitches getting the most circulation.

The Hillsdale baseball players were all in good moods, which was apparent to anyone they passed in the halls.

It was especially apparent to Lisa Cruz.

Lisa cornered Rob immediately on Friday morning during break.

"Hi, Rob," Lisa said, pulling him over to the side. "Nice game yesterday. That was great . . . you were great . . . and so was Hulk!"

"Uh, thanks, Lisa," Rob said, completely unaware of what was about to happen.

"So, I've been, uh, wondering, Rob," Lisa said shyly. "I . . . uh, . . . we uh, have been kinda' having fun in Science and stuff and uh . . ."

Rob stood silent, bewildered.

"Well . . . uh . . . I was wondering if you would . . . uh, go to Prom with me?" Lisa asked.

Rob went from bewildered to stunned to resigned. *Oh, man. I forgot this might happen. Now, I have to decide. Do I want to go? With Lisa? What about Allison? She can't go to Prom. Lisa can go to Prom . . . and she wants me to go. What about Allison? How can I say no? I don't want to hurt Lisa. I really like Lisa. But what about Allison? Me and Allison? No way!*

Rob had never thought so much, so fast, in his whole life.

"Oh, uh, geez, Lisa," Rob stumbled. "You really want to go with me?"

"Yes," Lisa said sincerely. "I think it would be fun. Jillian and Trip are going to go together . . . if we do . . . it will be great."

Oh yeah, Trip and Jillian, Rob realized. *I know Trip wants me to go. But what about Allison? Shut up! Why are you thinking about Allison? She's not your girlfriend!*

"Well, if you don't want to go," Lisa said, the hurt crushing her face.

"Oh, no," Rob said quickly. "That's not it at all . . . you just surprised me . . . sure . . . sure, I'll go with you. You really want me . . . me . . . to go with you??? You're a junior!"

"Yes, I want you to go," Lisa said, reverting to her shy way.

"OK, then . . . we'll go," Rob said softly.

"Oh, Rob . . . thanks," Lisa said with a huge smile.

Lisa then reached out and gave him a quick hug and pecked him on the cheek . . . and Rob was in swirling mode. *She kissed me,* he thought, as he smelled her perfume and felt her hands squeeze his arms.

"I'll let Jillian know so she and Trip can make their plans," Lisa squealed as she darted away. "Thanks, Rob . . . I'll see you in class!"

Rob stood shell-shocked, not quite knowing what had just happened.

Standing across the quad watching the couple, Allison Pierce also felt shell-shocked. *I'm not sure what just happened,* she thought . . . *but it looks like Rob just said yes to Lisa about Prom. I wish I had talked to Rob first . . . about him hugging me the other night . . . maybe he would have picked me as a girlfriend and said no to Lisa. I am such an idiot!!!*

CHAPTER 41
APRIL-SOPHOMORE YEAR

*T*HE weekend was spent honing Hulk's change-up, and Rob was so pleased with the progress on Sunday that he told Hulk he would recommend to Coach Wilson that Hulk get to use it on Monday against Milltown.

"You really think so?" Hulk questioned.

"Yeah," Rob answered emphatically. "You're ready!"

Hulk had almost danced away at the end of the practice at the "APF" . . . a somewhat funny sight to behold.

Allison Pierce was making her way over for "Movie Night" as Hulk pranced away, and she smiled at the sight.

"You've done a good job building him up, Rob Mathews," Allison said, almost shyly as she approached.

"Nah," Rob deferred. "He's got the talent . . . he did it himself."

Allison gave him a skeptical look, followed by a smile.

This is really awkward, they were both thinking.

"Uh, Rob," Allison began, squirming a bit.

Uh, oh, here it comes, Rob thought, squirming a little himself.

"I just wanted to thank you for the other night," Allison continued. "I really . . . really appreciated it."

"It's OK, Ally," Rob replied softly.

Ally . . . Ally . . . I love it when he calls me Ally!

"Those guys are just jerks," Rob added.

"I know, but . . . but you didn't have to come over and . . . and . . . hug me . . . like you did," Allison sputtered.

"Oh, uh, that was no big deal," Rob said, embarrassed about the hug.

"It was, too," Allison retorted. "It was a sweet thing to do . . . it really meant a lot . . . thank you."

"Oh, don't go all gooey on me now," Rob said with an uneasy laugh.

Allison paused and stared at Rob until he met her eye.

"Thank you, Rob," she said sincerely, flashing him her best smile.

"That's what friends are for, right," Rob said, trying hard to lighten the mood. "You know . . . that song . . . *You've Got a Friend* . . . by Carole King . . . come on, you remember!"

"I remember, Rob," Allison said softly, smiling at him again.

"HEY, YOU GUYS," Trip McHenry bellowed as he came up behind them. "This all looks pretty heavy . . . you guys need to be alone!"

"No, you jerk," Rob said quickly, thankful for an exit from his conversation with Allison.

"But, hey," Allison said to both guys, "now that you're both here . . . I wanted to ask you about the game Thursday. You guys both kept looking at me funny . . . were you trying to tell me something?"

"Yeah," Trip boomed. "We were telling you we were dedicating that game to you . . . because of those jerks . . . the Danielson's . . . you know."

Allison's face softened, and it looked like she might start crying. *Emily told me that was what it was . . . but to hear it from the guys is special.*

"Aw, that's so sweet, you guys," Allison said, and she moved to give them both a hug . . . but caught herself and just smiled at them through some light tears instead. *I think I love both these guys,* she thought suddenly . . . *but Rob the most!*

"Hey, Allison . . . what do you know . . . Rob's going to the Prom with Lisa!" Trip roared, trying to lighten the mood and shift the conversation. "How did you manage that?"

"Oh, just my Matchmaking 101 class skills," Allison retorted, quickly changing gears and trying to look happy with the news.

"Well, whatever you did, it worked!" Trip crowed. "Lisa asked him Friday . . . and he said yes . . . can you believe it! What's going to happen next year when he has to ask a girl to Prom on his own . . . what will you do then?"

"All right, that's enough," Rob grumbled. "Let's go eat and watch a movie . . . I'm starved."

I'm starved, too, Allison thought. *I love you so much, Rob Mathews! What will I do next year? I've got to come up with a plan for Rob to ask me to Prom. Good luck with that!*

***

MONDAY'S game against Milltown was another low-scoring nail-biter.

The Pirates struck early in the top of the 1st when Buck Buckman led off with a single, stole second, and scored on a Rob Mathews double off the wall.

Jose Rivera gave the run right back in the bottom half when he gave up his first home run of the year.

From there, the game became one of missed opportunities for Hillsdale, with very little offense from Milltown. The Pirates had runners in every inning, while Jose Rivera started dealing and blanked Milltown through five innings . . . except for that homer.

In the top of the 6th, Hillsdale struck paydirt, finally, when Rob, Trip, and Bruce Smithers blasted back-to-back-to-back doubles to plate a pair and give Hillsdale a 3-1 lead.

A tiring Jose Rivera skated around some minor trouble in the bottom of the 6th, and after a scoreless top of the 7th, it was Hulk Thomas time.

Facing the top of the order, Hulk made quick work of the leadoff hitter, inducing a weak grounder to short. The number two-hitter went out just as weakly on a pop fly to Trip McHenry in foul territory near the first base dugout.

Then came the number three-hitter, who had hit a monster home run against Hulk in their first meeting of the year.

Hulk sized him up and started him with a cutter on the inside corner for a strike. He went outside with a cutter and just missed for a 1-1 count.

Hulk went back outside with a cutter at the knees for a strike, then missed on a four-seamer above the letters and an inside cutter that just missed at the belt.

Hulk gathered himself behind the mound and peered out at Rob . . . they both nodded. Coach Wilson saw the exchange and flashed the sign for the change to Bruce Smithers.

C'mon' Hulk . . . throw a good pitch, Coach Wilson thought. *Don't overthrow it . . . relax and let it go!*

Hulk climbed up on the mound while the crowd from Hillsdale rose to their feet. Two out in the bottom of the 7th. Up 3-1, with a 3-2 count.

Hulk came set, rocked back, and fired. The change came out of his hand perfectly, and he watched as Milltown's slugger was utterly baffled. He started to swing . . . saw the changeup . . . tried to adjust . . . and waved weakly through it for strike three!

The Hillsdale crowd went crazy, with Grandpa Russell leading the cheers. Emily turned and gave Allison a big hug and high-fived her Dad while the rest of the Hillsdale crowd joined in the celebration.

Coach Wilson dashed to the mound to hug Hulk, and Rob joined him and the rest of the team.

"Hulk, Hulk," Coach Wilson shouted. "You are officially unhittable, Hulk . . . that was unreal!"

Hulk smiled broadly and headed for the dugout.

***

THE rest of April's schedule was a pair of shutouts, as the Pirates blanked Foothill 8-0 at home, and Taylor 6-0 on the road.

Hulk Thomas was unhittable in those games. Using his cutter and change consistently, he crossed up hitters right and left and piled up seven strikeouts in three innings of work without allowing a baserunner. He also noticed that the combination of the other two pitches made his four-seamer more effective.

Hulk, while still humble, was exuding confidence on the mound . . . and his teammates shared that confidence . . . and so did the Hillsdale fans, whose new favorite saying was "It's Hulk Thomas time!"

As April turned to May . . . with two weeks left in the regular season . . . Hillsdale had a polished and unhittable closer . . . ready to help Hillsdale win a title . . . as long as they could win out . . . and that included having to beat Cooley . . . and Pine Bluff!

Things were never easy . . .

CHAPTER 42
MAY-SOPHOMORE YEAR

MAY is the time of year in high school when the days fly by, especially for the seniors. There is a general excitement around all the senior activities . . . the senior trip, prom, graduation . . . it is a hectic time.

For Rob Mathews, early May of his sophomore year was also a hectic time. Three games the first week, working with Hulk at the "APF" on his change, driving lessons with Trip and Grandpa Russell . . . he and Trip both had appointments for their drivers test the Saturday morning before Prom. And, then there was the Prom . . . getting a tux, working out dinner plans, corsages . . . dancing lessons. Rob was glad that his Mom . . . and Allison . . . were helping him out!

To add to it, Rob talked Emily into hosting a special Sunday "Movie Night" . . . for the whole baseball team! There was going to be an afternoon BBQ and then a screening of *The Natural* in Rob's living room.

But first came the three league games.

Hillsdale started the week with a solid 9-2 victory at home against Oakville. Rob and Trip each homered, and Brad Wallace pitched a solid game . . . giving way to Hulk Thomas in the 7th to close the game out three up-three down.

Barker City again proved to be a formidable opponent. In the first, Hillsdale jumped out early on RBI singles from Trip McHenry and Bruce Smithers. Toby Tyler highlighted a four-run third inning with a monster home run to build the lead to 6-0.

Barker City clawed and scratched its way to single runs in the 4th, 5th, and 6th, off Jose Rivera, to make it 6-3 and set up Hulk Thomas time.

Hulk came in knowing he was facing the heart of the Barker City lineup . . . including the hitter who had blasted a monstrous three-run homer off them in Hillsdale.

But this was a different Hulk Thomas that the Mustangs had faced in their first meeting.

Hulk was in control of all three of his pitches . . . the four-seamer, the cutter, and the change . . . and he dazzled . . . and overpowered the Barker City hitters. The first hitter struck out on four pitches. The second on five . . . and the home run hitter weakly struck out swinging on a wicked change on the third pitch.

On Friday, the offense exploded, while Brad Wallace, Trip McHenry, and Hulk Thomas combined on a two-hit shutout to beat up on Colton by a 17-0 count. A Rob Mathews homer and five RBIs led the offense. Buck Buckman scored four runs, and Trip McHenry, Bruce Smithers, and Toby Tyler drove in a pair.

"Guys, you looked great this week. You worked hard in practice, and it showed," Coach Wilson said after the Colton game. "Next week . . . next week is the big week . . . we have Cooley and Pine Bluff . . . so we control our own destiny."

Coach Wilson paused again, looking beyond the team to see Dylan Cobb, a sophomore reporter for the school paper and the *Hillsdale Express,* standing on the dugout steps.

"Coach," Dylan said, hesitating to approach. "I've got some news . . ."

"What is it, Dylan?" Coach Wilson asked.

"Pine Bluff just lost to Cooley, 2-0," Dylan said, a smile playing over his lips.

Silence.

Then, a thunderous cheer from the whole team.

"Thanks, Dylan!" Coach Wilson called out, turning back to the team.

"OK," Coach Wilson said, digesting the news. "This clarifies things a little . . . maybe."

The Coach paused, thinking a minute before addressing the team again.

"So, here's what that means," Coach Wilson began. "We still control our destiny, of course . . . we win out, and we're champs."

Cheers from the team.

"We've got one loss . . . and so does Cooley," Coach Wilson continued. "Pine Bluff now has two losses."

Another round of cheers.

"Pine Bluff plays Colton Tuesday and us Thursday, Cooley plays us Tuesday and Colton Thursday . . . but let's be real . . . Cooley and Pine Bluff are both going to beat Colton," Coach Wilson explained.

Coach Wilson paused and pondered some more.

"The word is that only two teams will make the Sectionals from our league . . . unless there is a three-way tie . . . then all three will make it," Coach Wilson explained. "Cooley beats us . . . they're in . . . they'd have one loss with just Colton left to play."

The team sobered when hearing that.

"If we beat Cooley . . . we're in . . . and probably Cooley is in . . . because both teams could do no worse than a three-way tie for first . . . provided Cooley beats Colton . . . which they will. Pine Bluff would need to beat us to create a three-way tie." Coach Wilson said.

Heads were shaking in agreement.

"If we lose to Cooley . . . they're in . . . we would have two losses . . . Pine Bluff would have two losses . . . we'd be looking at a winner-take-all game on Friday against Pine Bluff," Coach Wilson added.

"Ahem," Trip cleared his throat. "I say we just beat both of them . . . that makes us champs by ourselves . . . and leaves Pine Bluff out of Sectionals! Now that would be sweet!"

"Exactly my plan," Coach Wilson laughed amid a huge cheer. "Exactly my plan."

CHAPTER 43
MAY-SOPHOMORE YEAR

*A***LLISON** Pierce smiled as she watched the baseball team play a whiffle ball game at the "APF" Saturday afternoon. *The guys are all so relaxed . . . they're having so much fun . . . it's not like it is in a real game,* she realized.

She gazed around the yard and spotted Grandma and Grandpa Russell sitting on the front porch with big, contented smiles. *They sure love Rob,* Allison thought. *They sure love seeing him enjoy himself. I think they love Trip, too . . . especially Grandpa.*

Allison continued to scan the backyard and saw Emily . . . standing near the BBQ, watching Coach Wilson grill burgers and hotdogs. Their easy banter put a smile on Allison's face. *They are a good couple,* she mused. *Another match by the Matchmaker queen! I wonder when Emily will be ready?*

Allison's Mom, Linda, joined the picture, carrying a tray of buns and heavy paper plates out to the grill, and Coach Wilson shouted a ten-minute warning to the guys.

***

*W***ITH** dinner over, and the grill, the yard, and the dishes cleaned and garbage thrown away, 18 teenage boys, Allison and Linda Pierce, Emily and Dave Wilson, crowded into the living room to watch the movie. Grandpa and Grandma Russell had taken one quick look . . . and smell . . . of the room and had hit the exit door.

Allison had been a little miffed at this intrusion into "Movie Night"... not only changing it from Sunday to Saturday... but she had been hoping for a little alone time with Rob. *I can't help but think something's changed,* she pondered. *Rob does seem different somehow... he seems to treat me a little differently. Is that good or bad?*

But now, sitting in the middle of a pile of sweaty, dirty, smelly boys, she was loving it. As *The Natural* unfolded, she was drawn into the movie and entranced by the story of good and evil with the baseball backdrop. She cheered when the hero hit the game-winning home run and cried when he played catch with his newly reunited son. *That was a good movie,* she thought.

When the movie ended, the guys hung out, and Allison was included... this was a young team... and she had known most of them since they were in elementary school. Since the movie was a long one... and it was getting late, the guys started peeling off as parents showed up to fetch them, or those close enough to walk headed home.

Soon, it was just Trip, who was spending the night, and Rob, sitting with Allison on the front porch, while Linda, Dave, and Emily sat around the island in the kitchen.

"So, what do you think about your Mom and Coach Wilson, Rob?" Trip asked abruptly.

Allison cringed immediately. *Don't blow this, Trip!*

"Huh?" Rob asked quickly. "What about them?"

"It seems like they are hitting it off pretty well," Trip grinned. "I think it's kinda' cool."

"You think so?" Rob asked. "I didn't notice anything."

"That's because you were too busy trying to win that whiffle ball game," Trip laughed.

"Really?" Rob exclaimed. "Allison... what... did you see anything?"

"Oh, they were just being nice... you know," Allison said lightly.

Trip looked at her and realized he should tread lightly.

"Yeah, nothing big," Trip added. "Just looked like they were having fun talking."

"Hmmm," Rob mused. "Mom and Coach Wilson . . . that would be cool!" *Would it?* Rob paused and thought it through. *Yeah, it would be cool. I know Mom likes him . . . I wonder if she's ready?*

"Really?" Allison responded with surprise.

"Yeah . . . really," Rob replied thoughtfully. "I know she's going to get married again someday . . . and I'm going to have a Step-Dad . . . so, if it's going to happen anyway . . . having Coach as my Step-Dad would be nice. He's a good guy, a good role model . . . I think he'd be good for Mom."

"Oh, Rob, that's great," Allison said enthusiastically. "I've been working on your Mom and Coach . . . but knowing you're OK with it . . . well, that makes it better."

"What are you, the Mathews Family Personal Matchmaker?" Trip laughed loudly.

Just as the kid's laughter died down, the front door swung open and out walked the adults.

Linda Pierce was the first to peel off.

"Thanks for dinner and the movie, Emily . . . and you, too, Dave. The food was delicious."

Emily and Dave both mumbled their thanks.

"Allison, I'm heading home . . . don't stay too much longer. These folks need their sleep . . . a big week coming up. Big games . . . the Prom . . ."

The boys laughed nervously.

Oh. Geez, the Prom, Rob instantly thought. *I need dance lessons.*

"OK, Mom, I'll be home soon," Allison replied.

"Well, guys . . . and Allison . . . see you on Monday," Coach Wilson said. "You guys make sure you get some sleep . . . you'll need your rest . . . for all that dancing on Saturday!"

Everyone laughed hard . . . except Rob.

"Emily," Coach Wilson said, turning back to Rob's Mom. "Thanks for a fun evening. I can see why the guys always say how welcome you make them feel. That's a gift. Thanks for letting me share in that!"

Emily smiled graciously, looked down briefly, then lifted her head back to Coach Wilson.

"And, thank you, Dave . . . for doing all the cooking . . . and all the cleanup," Emily said sincerely. "It was a fun night."

The pair shared a long look, and then Coach Wilson snapped back.

"OK, see you all later," Coach Wilson said with a wave.

"And I hope to see you Tuesday at the game, Emily," he quipped to Emily.

"Oh, I think I'll be there," Emily said softly, watching Coach Wilson walk to the street, hop in his car, and drive away with a quick wave.

Emily watched as the car turned the corner, sighed softly, and looked down to see the three kids staring at her.

"What?" Emily asked, flustered at being caught. "What?"

"Nothing, Mom," Rob smiled. "Nothing at all."

Allison and Trip both smiled that smile . . . the one that says they knew something.

"Oh, stop," Emily said firmly. "I'm not ready to start dating."

"Wait . . . what?" Rob asked sarcastically. "I don't know what you mean . . . dating?"

"Oh, you guys . . . don't be out here too late keeping the neighbors awake," Emily said quickly and darted into the house.

"I think she's close to being ready," Allison said knowingly.

"Looks that way," Trip said.

"Yeah, it does," Rob said. *The question is . . . am I ready? Yeah . . . I think so.*

CHAPTER 44
MAY-SOPHOMORE YEAR

*T*HE threesome sat and talked for a while . . . it was Saturday, so they could stay up late, and the evening was a little brisk but pleasant.

Around 11:30, Trip stood and stretched and said, "I think I'm beat, guys . . . I'm going to head into bed. Night."

"Good night, Trip," Allison said, while Rob just said, "Night."

Allison and Rob sat for a couple of minutes just thinking.

Rob broke the silence by saying, "You think my Mom's ready to date?"

"She's close . . . it's been almost two years . . ." Allison replied softly, her voice trailing off.

"Yeah, in a couple of months," Rob said, the memory of his Dad's death choking him up.

"Are you ready for it, Rob?" Allison asked gently.

Rob paused a moment.

"Yeah, I am," he finally said. "It's been long enough . . . and I don't want to see her miss her chance . . . and Coach is a great guy."

"Yes, he is," Allison said. *And so are you,* she thought.

They both sat in silence for a long moment.

"Well, I better head home, too," Allison said.

Rob got up with her and followed her down the walkway.

"I'll walk you home," Rob said, feeling incredibly close to Allison at the moment.

They walked silently until she went up her porch stairs and turned back to him.

"Rob, thanks again," Allison began. "Thanks for being my friend."

Rob looked up at her, she flashed him her killer smile, and he melted.

"Aw, you're more than a friend, Ally . . ." Rob said.

Ally . . . Ally . . . I love it . . . what is he going to say next?

Rob appeared flustered and finally said. "Well . . . you're my best friend . . ."

Allison beamed at him, and he smiled back, neither of them sure what to do or say next.

"And," Rob mustered, "my dance teacher! You promised me a lesson before the Prom."

That broke the spell.

They both laughed.

"You got it," Allison chirped, wishing he would have professed his everlasting love instead. *But, hey, at least I'll get to dance with him . . . and he'll hold me. Maybe someday he'll say it . . . ask me out . . . maybe someday I'll be something more than just his best friend.*

"When and where?" Allison asked.

"Maybe your house . . . maybe Saturday afternoon," Rob answered.

"I'll be there," Allison said and went inside to shed some tears of joy and a little remorse.

***

ROB opened his front door, closed it behind him, and locked up for the night. He was heading upstairs when he noticed a light in the den. Rob saw his Mom sitting on the little couch, thumbing through some old photos with a misty look on her face.

"You OK, Mom?" Rob asked with concern.

Emily looked startled, and Rob noticed a few tears in her eyes.

"Mom, you OK?" he asked again, moving toward her.

"Yes, yes, I'm fine, Rob," Emily said with a trace of embarrassment. "Just reminiscing."

"Mom," Rob said, "you know . . . I want you to know . . . when you're ready to date . . . I'm OK with it."

Emily started to protest.

"I know you're not ready," Rob interjected. "But when you are, I'm OK . . . and I'm OK if you're ready now."

Emily smiled through growing tears.

"I'm . . . I'm not quite ready, Rob, but I'm getting close," Emily sputtered. "I know your Dad would have wanted me to move on . . . he wouldn't want me being alone forever."

"I know, Mom," Rob responded, and Emily got up from the couch and held out her arms.

She hugged him tightly and then pushed back from him and said, "So . . . if and when I do date . . . do you . . . do you think it's OK for me to date Coach Wilson?"

"When you're ready, Mom," Rob said, looking into her eyes and smiling. "Yeah, it's OK with me . . . I don't want you to miss any chance to be happy! Especially with Coach!"

Emily pulled him close for another hug.

***

THE headline in the Sunday morning *Hillsdale Express* said it all:

MAKE OR BREAK WEEK FOR THREE TEAMS

IN HIGH SCHOOL BASEBALL CHAMPIONSHIP FIGHT

"Boy, they have that right, don't they," Grandpa Russell said as he showed the headline to Rob and Trip as they sat down at the table for Sunday breakfast.

Rob and Trip nodded and said their morning hellos to Emily and Grandma Russell.

"What'd the "Old Grump" say this morning?" Rob asked.

"Not a lot," Grandpa Russell relayed. "Dylan Cobb did a huge story . . . well done . . . I think he's going to be a good writer."

The boys nodded.

"So, Dan Mercer has a blurb in his column . . . want to hear it?" Grandpa Russell asked, thumbing through the paper to find it . . . knowing the boys would say yes.

They nodded again as Emily put heaping plates of bacon, eggs, and toast in front of them.

"Ahem," Grandpa Russell began. "So, here we are at the pivotal week in the baseball season for Hillsdale High. It's been a strange season thus far . . . awesome pitching and defense . . . except for a few blown games here and there. Awesome offense from Buck Buckman, Rob Mathews, and a host of others . . . but a real lack of "in the clutch" hitting in critical situations."

Grandpa Russell paused, and smiled at the mention of Rob's name, and then continued reading out loud.

"And that's the key to the week . . . if Hillsdale wins one of their two games . . . they're in the playoffs. If they beat Cooley, they're in . . . if they lose to Cooley . . . well, they would likely have a sudden death playoff with Pine Bluff for the last spot in the Sectionals. The real question is . . . can they come through in the clutch . . . I'm betting yes."

CHAPTER 45
MAY-SOPHOMORE YEAR

***S**PRING* had sprung . . . so much so that as Hillsdale readied themselves at home on Tuesday against Cooley, the temperature sat at an even 80 degrees.

The bleachers were packed for the Pirate's last "official" home game of the year. "Official" because to get another home game, they had to go to the Sectionals . . . with the Semifinals and Finals again being held at Hillsdale's complex.

With the last home game came Senior Day, where the seniors and their families were honored before the game. Touching scenes played out . . . but all of the players . . . seniors included . . . just wanted to get this show on the road.

At last, the festivities were over, and Jose Rivera was completing his warmups for the most significant start of his young life . . . a chance to nail down no worse than a piece of a championship for Hillsdale . . . and a spot in the Sectionals.

Rob Mathews scanned the stands . . . everywhere he looked were people he knew. His family . . . out in full force . . . all of the Pierce's, Trip's Aunt Barb and her kids, Phil Boyer and Stephanie Miller, Bill Tompkins and Kenny Anderson, Dee Dee Baker and Don Harbin . . . Donnie Fields and Christina Craft . . . and Lisa Cruz . . . who was sitting with Allison and his family!

So, the huge roar of the hometown crowd did not surprise him as the Pirates took the field to the strains of *Centerfield* by John Fogerty, which spoke to Rob on every level. *Let's do this!*

***

JOSE Rivera came out smoking hot. He sliced through the top three Cooley hitters on just eight pitches.

But Cooley's southpaw ace, Seth Gardner, nearly matched him. It took Seth ten pitches to get through the first, retiring Buck Buckman on a grounder to third, Mark Porter on a pop to second, and Rob Mathews on a sinking liner to center.

"Might be one of those days," Grandpa Russell moaned as Rob's "sure hit" was taken away on a nice running catch.

The crowd sensed the same thing, and the tension immediately started to mount. The feeling grew as both lefties continued to mow hitters down.

Jose Rivera was perfect through four innings . . . but so was Seth Gardner, and the crowd was getting restless on both sides of the diamond . . . the fans wanted some offense, and they wanted it now!

It came out of nowhere . . . on the first pitch of the top of the 5th inning. Jose Rivera tried to steal a strike against Cooley's number four-hitter . . . and he hung a curve ball out over the middle of the plate.

The ball was gone in a blink . . . deposited far over the left-center field fence . . . and there went the perfect game, the no-hitter, and the shutout. Cooley 1, Hillsdale 0.

While the Cooley fans went ballistic, an uneasy feeling started to creep over the Hillsdale side of the field.

"No problem," Rob shouted as he entered the dugout at the end of the half-inning. "We need at least one to win . . . nobody wins if they can't score. Come on, Trip, start us off."

Many Hillsdale fans were thinking, *can we get even one?*

Not in the bottom of 5th. Trip lined out, Bruce Smithers grounded out, Toby Tyler struck out . . . and Seth Gardner was perfect through five.

Back out for the 6th was Jose Rivera. The slender left-hander was still looking strong, so Coach Wilson was sticking with him . . . and he was glad he did when Jose delivered a stellar inning, getting three quick outs . . . getting Hillsdale back to the dugout, ready to hit.

But Seth Gardner had other ideas . . . and he struck out Matt Bryant on four pitches, Josh Lee on five, and Gavin Ford on three. Still perfect. End of six.

Coach Wilson was trying to figure out what to do. He had Hulk Thomas loose and ready in the bullpen . . . but no lead to protect . . . and a starting pitcher, Jose Rivera, who had only given up just the one hit . . . the one baserunner . . . the one run.

The Coach took off his hat and ran his hands through his sandy, blond hair. *Do I bring in Hulk or leave Jose? A long pause. No . . . stick with Jose . . . we can use Hulk later if we need to . . . but why show the Cooley hitters Hulk and his changeup now, with no lead to protect? We may see these guys in the playoffs. Yeah . . . stick with Jose.*

So, out to the mound went Jose Rivera. No one on the Hillsdale side was happier than Coach Wilson when Jose went through Cooley 1-2-3 . . . and brought Hillsdale to the plate with one last chance . . . and the top of the order coming up.

CHAPTER 46
MAY-SOPHOMORE YEAR

"*RALLY* CAP TIME!!!" Grandpa Russell bellowed. Amazingly, a good portion of the crowd indulged him, and they started to get loud. They got even louder when Buck Buckman drilled a solid shot to center field on the first pitch of the bottom of the 7th!

"YAHOO!!!" crowed Grandpa Russell. "I told you . . . they work every time!!! I knew he couldn't keep this offense down forever."

Now hope rose, as Buck Buckman promptly stole second on the first pitch to Mark Porter . . . tying run at second . . . no outs.

Hope was dashed immediately when Mark Porter popped his sacrifice bunt attempt straight up for out number one.

"Aw," Allison said grimly. "Do you think they'll walk Rob now, Grandpa . . . first base is open . . . they're probably too scared to pitch to him."

"No, they won't want to put the winning run on base," Grandpa Russell lectured. "One of the golden rules . . . don't put the winning run on for free . . ."

Allison gulped. *I wish they would walk Rob . . . it will be so hard if he doesn't come through . . . but then it would be up to Trip. Oh . . . please, one of you, come through!*

Rob strode confidently to the plate. *He's not going to give in here . . . gotta' look for pitches on the black or just off the plate . . . go with the pitch,* he thought.

Strike one. A backdoor-breaking pitch that just caught the outside corner.

Ball one, inside at the knees.

Strike two . . . fastball at the letters . . . caught Rob guessing.

C'mon, idiot, Rob berated himself. *You can't be guessing now. Take what he gives you. Go with the pitch.*

"Oh no," Allison cried out. *Please . . . please . . . please get a hit.*

Next to her, both Grandpa Russell and Emily were thinking the same thing. Time seemed to stand still.

Seth Gardner toes the rubber. Fires pitch number four . . . just inside . . . ball two . . . 2-2 count. One out, Buck at 2nd.

Gardner climbs back to the mound. Fires to the plate. Backdoor breaking pitch.

Rob times it. Keeps his weight back. Sees the ball breaking back toward the strike zone. Moves into the pitch. *Hit it to right . . . hard,* Rob thinks.

"PING!!!!"

The ball jumped off Rob's bat on a line toward right field.

The first baseman jumped . . . over his head. Buck, at second, sees the ball clear the first baseman and can see the right fielder is too deep to catch it on the fly. Base hit!!!

Buck is off like a shot, exploding around third and heading for home and a tie game.

Rob hustles to first and rounds it tightly . . . unsure of whether the first baseman will allow the ball to go through to the plate or not.

The right fielder's throw is on a line. The first baseman lets the ball go through . . . but Rob is forced to stay at first.

Buck is dashing for the plate . . . the throw is online . . . it's going to be close!

CHAPTER 47
MAY-SOPHOMORE YEAR

"**Y**ER' out!!!!!" screams the umpire, and the Cooley side of the field goes crazy.

Hillsdale's fans are stunned. Hillsdale players are stunned. Allison, Emily, and Grandpa Russell feel like they have been kicked in the gut.

"NOOOOO!!!!!" they all scream.

Two outs. Rob Mathews at first. Trip McHenry coming up. Last chance.

"C'mon', Trip," Rob shouts out from first. "You're the man. Keep us going!"

Trip takes a strike. A ball. Another ball. A screaming line drive...just foul. Another ball. 3-2 count. Fans all on their feet. You cannot hear yourself think.

Seth Gardner sets. Looks at Rob. Goes to the plate. Rob off on movement. Ball headed to the plate.

"PING!!!!"

Smashed into to left center. Ball dropping. Base hit. Left fielder with the ball... throwing to third...Rob closing in on third...ball's there...Rob's there...SAFE!!!

In the commotion at third, Trip McHenry scrambles into second. Two outs. Second and third. 1-0 Cooley. Bruce Smithers up.

Bruce Smithers to first. Intentional walk. Bases loaded. Two outs. Toby Tyler strides to the plate.

First pitch. PING!!!!

Another rocket . . . heading for the gap in left-center . . . it drops, Hillsdale wins . . . if not . . . game over, 1-0 Cooley.

The center fielder is racing to his glove hand . . . Rob has crossed the plate, and Trip is rounding third . . .

The center fielder dives headlong . . . the ball disappears into his glove . . . he rolls over . . . looks around . . . he opens his glove . . . shows the ump the ball . . .

"Yer' out!!!" bellows the ump.

Cooley goes wild. The Hillsdale players all stop in mid-stride . . . and stare in disbelief.

The Hillsdale crowd exhales and deflates as one. One second, they were standing and screaming in joy . . . and the next second, they were sitting holding their faces in their hands in utter disbelief . . . and sorrow.

Rob, who had made it home in time to turn around and see the catch, could not believe his eyes . . . he stood there numbly, watching Cooley celebrating their first championship . . . at least a share of the championship . . . in 20 years . . . and their first spot in the Sectionals in 12 years.

Bewildered, Trip walked the last few steps to the plate and stood on it just to be safe.

"What happened . . . how did he catch that?" Trip asked. "I didn't think he had a chance."

"I don't know . . ." Rob sputtered. "I just don't know."

The big Cooley crowd, who had journeyed to Hillsdale hoping to do just this, rushed the field. Rob knew firsthand how much fun they were having . . . and how hard it was to be in Hillsdale's shoes.

He and Trip watched with dismay as the Cooley players were swarmed by their friends, family, and teammates and started to party!

"I just don't know how that happened," Rob said again. "That should be us out there celebrating."

"I know," Trip said. "I can't believe it."

"That'll be us on Friday in Pine Bluff," Rob said defiantly.

Trip looked at him in wonder.

"I believe you, "Wonder Boy," Trip said with a half-hearted smile. "I believe you . . . you and I need to make sure that happens."

"Done," said Rob, with determination etched on his face.

CHAPTER 48
MAY-SOPHOMORE YEAR

COOLEY was still partying 20 minutes later... but it was starting to break up. The Hillsdale team had finished their talk... and started drifting off one by one.

Rob Mathews sat alone now in the dugout, staring into space. *This is not what was supposed to happen... how did we lose to Cooley... twice in one year? They aren't better than we are... we have the better team... how did this happen?*

He put his face in his hands and took a deep breath. *This isn't as bad as the "Pick" games ... or losing Dad... but... I'll get it through it. But it hurts.*

He felt, rather than saw, somebody sitting heavily down on the bench next to him.

"Here we are again," drawled Coach Wilson.

Rob looked up.

"Yeah... we have to stop meeting like this," Rob said in a low voice.

Coach Wilson laughed, a dry, mirthless laugh.

"Agreed," he said, sitting back and following Rob's gaze out onto the field... where the last remnants of the victorious Cooley Cougars were finally leaving.

"We'll get them in Sectionals," Rob spouted. "Nobody beats us three times in one year!"

Coach Wilson smiled at Rob's confidence.

"You forgetting about Pine Bluff?" Coach Wilson asked. "They might have something to say about whether we make the Sectionals or not."

"Don't worry about Pine Bluff," Trip McHenry boomed from the dugout steps.

Coach Wilson and Rob looked up to see Trip McHenry moving their way.

"I don't like those Danielson boys," Trip boomed again. "We're not losing to Pine Bluff ever again . . . at anything!"

Rob rolled his eyes at Coach Wilson, and they both laughed without much conviction.

"Valley Christian . . . the same thing . . ." Trip continued. "We're done losing to them, too."

"How about Cooley?" Coach Wilson asked.

"That's a tough one," Trip said. "Cooley . . . they got a bunch of nice guys . . . that Gardner . . . he's got class . . . can't seem to get too worked up about them."

"Maybe that's the problem," Coach Wilson said with a slight twinkle in his eye.

That stopped Trip short, and they all paused for a moment.

"Well . . . Pine Bluff on Friday," Coach Wilson said as he stood and moved to take off. "We going to beat Pine Bluff?"

"Guaranteed," Trip answered immediately.

"Rob?" Coach Wilson asked.

"Guaranteed," said Rob, his mouth set in determination.

"I'll let the press know," Coach Wilson said with a laugh, gauging the boy's reaction.

"Fine by me," they both said at the same time.

"Hey, I'm taking off . . . gotta' new girl to meet," Trip said. "You OK?"

"Yeah," Rob answered. "I'm OK. I'll feel better after our guaranteed win on Friday!"

"Yeah, me too," Trip said sheepishly as he bounded up the stairs. "One of these days, my mouth is going to get me in trouble."

"One of these days?" Rob joked.

"Yeah, one of these days . . . but not today," Trip shouted back at Rob as he left the dugout.

Rob felt better . . . but still put his hands back over his face and rubbed lightly. He raised his head, pulled his hands away, and all he saw was a beautiful early evening at the ballpark. *I love it here . . . well, maybe not as much as usual right now!*

"Rob?" a quiet voice broke Rob's concentration on the field before him.

Rob looked up and saw Allison standing at the top of the dugout steps . . . not sure if she should come down them or not.

"Hey, Allison," Rob said, motioning her to come down.

Allison timidly approached and sat down.

"I thought you had something important right after the game tonight?" Rob asked her as she sat down next to him.

"Yeah . . . I do . . . I've got a meeting to get to . . ." Allison said. "But . . . I just wanted to check and make sure you were OK . . . that was brutal."

"Yeah," Rob sighed. "Sometimes, I think it's harder to watch that kind of thing," Rob said. "You know my Mom . . . Grandpa Russell . . . and you . . . just to watch and not be able to do anything to help . . ."

"I know," Allison said, with a hint of a smile. "I kind of live and die with this stuff now, too . . ."

"Yeah, who'd a thunk," Rob teased. "Allison Pierce . . . "spooorts" junkie!"

"Yeah, who indeed," she replied.

Rob looked back out on the field, and they were silent for a long moment.

"Anyway..." Allison began, "I thought I'd make sure you were OK... thought, maybe ... you know... if you needed one... I could pay back your hug."

Rob turned quickly to Allison in surprise, thinking she was joking... but he saw immediately she was being sincere.

He gazed at her, and she gave him a small smile.

"It seems like the least I could do," she stammered. "You know... for my best friend. I wanted to make sure you knew... you know... *You've Got a Friend*... by Carole King ... you know... the song."

"Yeah, I know... the song," Rob said.

"So?" Allison prodded.

Rob stood and faced her... and reached down and helped her up, looking her in the eyes.

"You know," Rob said shakily. "I think I could use a hug from a friend."

Allison smiled her best smile, reached around him, and pulled him close.

Rob immediately felt an electric charge go through him... like the feeling he remembered with Stephanie Miller. *Whoa*, he thought. *What was that? With Allison?*

He pulled her closer... she smelled and felt so good. *What is going on?*

Allison nestled in tighter, and they both felt the same thing. Neither one wanted it to stop ... and the length of the hug started to get awkward.

Finally, and reluctantly, Rob pulled away and looked down at Allison.

"Well, if I had to have a hug from a friend, I'm glad it was you and not Trip," Rob laughed.

Allison broke up and started giggling.

"Me, too," she said after she calmed down. "Me, too!"

CHAPTER 49
MAY-SOPHOMORE YEAR

WEDNESDAY turned out to be a pretty somber day until after lunch. The mood for the baseball team . . . and a lot of the school . . . and town . . . was one of stunned disbelief.

The gnawing in Rob's stomach was not from hunger but was that feeling you get after you've been punched in the stomach.

Other students picked up on the mood and gave the team a wide berth . . . until Science class right after lunch.

Allison Pierce and Lisa Cruz made a difference for Rob . . . and for Trip . . . by starting up a running banter after they broke into small group study.

The four of them were grouped, and Allison immediately steered the conversation away from sports and on to anything else. Lisa picked up on it, and it became a game to stay away from sports or instantly change the subject if sports came up in the conversation.

At first, Rob and Trip were annoyed, but they soon understood what the girls were doing and started playing along. Several times the teacher had to hush the foursome to stop the giggling.

Rob reflected as he sat watching Allison and Lisa. *They are both really funny . . . both so smart . . . and both very sweet. I really like Lisa,* Rob thought. *She's not beautiful like Stephanie Miller is . . . but she's just cute and fun . . . I think this Prom thing is going to be OK with Lisa . . . we'll have fun.*

But as he sat back and enjoyed the girls, his thoughts immediately went to Allison. *She's such a geek. But the other day . . . with her glasses off . . . her eyes were really beautiful . . . and she really is beautiful inside. And those hugs . . . that feeling when we hugged . . . it was electric.*

On and on it went during Science, and by the end of the class, he was not only feeling much better . . . but was totally confused over how he felt about Lisa . . . and Allison.

**

COACH Wilson had asked Rob to suspend the extra workouts at the "APF" for the next few days.

"I just want you all to relax a little bit," he explained.

It worked out great for Rob and Trip, allowing them extra driving time with Grandpa Russell.

The three of them were enjoying their drive time together . . . especially Grandpa Russell, who used the time to get his "Sports Talk" in without annoying Grandma Russell.

It was clear Grandpa Russell had taken a genuine interest in Trip, and that Trip looked up to . . . and enjoyed Grandpa Russell immensely.

As they drove, they talked a lot about their summer baseball trip . . . now less than a month away, and about sports in general. Grandpa Russell also discovered ways to drop in comments or hints about leading a good life and doing the right thing.

While Rob was driving back to the house Wednesday evening, he pulled up to a stoplight along the main highway, came to a stop, and looked to his left to see Tony Russo pull up next to him in his fancy sports car.

Tony noticed him at once and immediately put his passenger side window down . . . Rob's window was already open.

"Wow!" Tony exclaimed. "They really let losers like you drive!"

Rob just turned away and stared straight out the window, waiting for the light to change.

"Tell me, Mathews," Tony continued. "How did you guys lose to Cooley . . . twice?!!!"

Rob stared straight ahead.

Tony burst out laughing . . . hard . . . and continued it until he saw Trip McHenry put his window down and say, "That's what they are going to be asking you when we beat you in Sectionals!"

Tony laughed hard again.

"You guys won't even make Sectionals . . . if you can't beat Cooley, how are you going to beat Pine Bluff!!!" Tony needled.

"See you, losers!!!" Tony shouted as the light changed, and he sped away.

Rob glanced at his Grandpa and, in the rearview mirror, to see Trip hanging his head.

"What's wrong, Trip?" Rob asked.

"I better stop saying stuff like that," Trip said. "It may come back to haunt us."

Rob nodded in agreement . . . and then smiled and said, "But, it will be very sweet . . . when we beat them."

CHAPTER 50
MAY-SOPHOMORE YEAR

FRIDAY finally arrived, and brought with it, bright and early . . . Rob's butterflies. The feeling in his stomach had changed from a gut punch to that gnawing knot of anxiety . . . and impatience to get this game started.

His mind was also filled with everything else happening this weekend. Besides the game, Rob had his Driver's test and the Prom . . . and a dance lesson with Allison! Strangely, Rob was looking forward to his dance lesson more than anything!

But . . . first things first . . . the do-or-die game with Pine Bluff.

Funny, Rob thought as he showered and dressed for school. *I never . . . ever . . . would have thought we would have to beat Pine Bluff just to make the playoffs! I just assumed we'd be champs again this year.*

But here they were, fighting to extend their season . . . and having to do it on Pine Bluff's home diamond . . . a tall order.

The bus ride to Pine Bluff was subdued. The whole team knew the importance of this game, and some of the younger kids who hadn't been through it before looked nervous. Josh Lee looked good . . . he had been through it during the basketball season . . . while Hulk Thomas seemed a bit nervous . . . but . . . confident and ready.

Getting off the bus . . . and onto the field was a big help, and Rob could see some of those nerves go away. *But will they come back at a crucial time? I hope not,* he thought.

***

THE huge crowd was settling in . . . it was standing room only, and fans crowded along the foul line fences, and anywhere else they could get a view.

Today was Senior Day for Pine Bluff, and Rob realized . . . *this could be Jeb Danielson's last high school game ever . . . in any sport . . . and I'd love to send him out as a loser.*

As Rob warmed up down the third base line, he searched the crowd for his family and friends, finally finding them about halfway up near third base. Everyone had made the trip to Pine Bluff . . . and there sat Allison Pierce, of course . . . and Lisa Cruz . . . sitting with his Mom.

What does Mom think of Lisa? Rob mused as his pregame warmup ended. *I bet she likes her . . . she's a nice girl. But . . . so is Allison . . . she is so special! Just stop thinking about girls . . . about Allison . . . focus on the game!*

During the quick Senior Day program, Rob saw Jeb's parents on the field for the ceremony. W*eird to think that Jeb Danielson has parents,* Rob mused. *Enough already . . . it's time to focus!*

After the festivities, the Warriors quickly raced out onto the field . . . and Jeb Danielson climbed onto the mound and readied to throw the first pitch. He was focused.

It is evident from that first pitch that Jeb Danielson was all business today. He snapped off a wicked slider for strike one to Buck Buckman and got better from there.

Three pitches and Buck was done . . . Mark Porter followed suit with a three-pitch strikeout, not making contact, and Rob Mathews popped one up sky-high to Clem Danielson at shortstop. Three up, three down.

"Just missed it," Rob told Trip as he went to get his glove.

"Yeah . . ." Trip quipped sarcastically, "I thought it was gone . . ."

But Rob was serious. *A quarter-inch difference and that ball was out of here,* Rob thought with a grimace.

Rob was also serious about his pitching. He matched Clem's performance retiring the first three in order on just six pitches, including a three-pitch strikeout of Clem Danielson, hitting in the number two-slot today.

And, so it went. Similar to the Cooley game, both pitchers were dominant. A ton of swing-throughs, weak ground balls, and soft pop flies were the order of the day.

The huge crowd on both sides of the field started getting restless early on, both sides lusting for a breakthrough to put their team on top.

Through three innings, both pitchers were still perfect. Through four innings... through five... not a single baserunner.

"No!!!!" the Pine Bluff side groaned as Buck Buckman made a sensational running catch to keep Rob perfect to end the 5th inning.

"Oh, please, please, please," hundreds of Hillsdale fans prayed as the Pirates came to hit in the 6th inning.

"We've got to get something going here," Grandpa Russell bellowed to be heard above the crowd. "RALLY CAPS, EVERYBODY!!!"

Allison looked at Lisa and smiled.

"I love Grandpa Russell," Allison said to Lisa.

Lisa rolled her eyes and laughed... but both girls pulled off their caps, turned them inside out, put them on backwards, and started cheering for Matt Bryant to get a hit.

It was not to be. Jeb Danielson continued to deal, quickly working through the bottom three of the Hillsdale order.

Rob, determination oozing, took the mound in the bottom half... and struck out the side!

Both pitchers were 18 up and 18 down. Not a single baserunner.

It was obvious... to even the casual fan that both pitchers had even better stuff and more determination against certain hitters.

For Jeb Danielson, his battles against Rob Mathews and Trip McHenry were... simply put... wars. His face would grow dark when they approached the plate... his velocity would increase, and his pitches had a sharper break... and his smile was broader each time he retired them.

Rob's face was a mask. He wore the same expression no matter who he faced, but like Jeb, his velocity and movement elevated when he faced the three Danielson boys... and there was a trace of a smile when they trudged back to the bench.

The pitcher's lines were eerily similar. Both had struck out nine, had four ground ball outs, and five in the air. Neither had gone to a 3-ball count of any kind. And both were determined to stay perfect.

Going to the top of the 7th... scoreless perfection. Winner goes to the Sectionals. Losers are done for the season.

Which pitcher would flinch first?

CHAPTER 51
MAY-SOPHOMORE YEAR

***J**EB* Danielson flinched first. The perfect game was history on the first pitch of the top of the 7th inning.

Buck Buckman rifled a clean single to right center, and the Hillsdale crowd exploded.

Jeb Danielson looked like he might explode as well.

On the first pitch to Mark Porter, he reared back at threw his hardest pitch of the day. Mark bunted it about 15 feet in front of the plate, and Buck took off for second base.

Jeb Danielson crashed in off the mound, fielded the ball cleanly, and looked at second . . . no chance there . . . so he turned to throw to first . . . and no one was there.

The second baseman was on his way . . . but he was late. Jeb tried to lead him perfectly . . . but his throw was too hard and skipped past first into short right field.

Buck and Mark took advantage, and each took another base, and Hillsdale was in business with runners at 2nd and 3rd, no one out . . . and Rob Mathews coming to the plate.

The Hillsdale fans, still with their Rally Caps in position, were on their feet, screaming as loud as they could.

"Will they let Rob hit?" Allison screamed to Grandpa Russell. "They won't walk him, right? Don't want to put another run on base."

"Afraid not," Grandpa Russell screamed back. "Different rule. They're not protecting a lead . . . they'll walk him to set up a force anywhere . . . much easier to get out of a bases-loaded jam than second and third."

Allison nodded and watched Pine Bluff's head coach talk with Jeb Danielson.

"You know they're going to walk me, don't you," Rob Mathews said to Trip McHenry.

Trip nodded.

"You know what you're going to do, don't you," Rob smiled.

Trip nodded.

The meeting on the mound went on for a long minute and was definitely an argument between the coach . . . and his ace pitcher. The coach won . . . and the next thing you knew, Rob Mathews was jogging down to first base.

Bases loaded. No outs. No score.

Trip McHenry coming up to hit.

Jeb Danielson was seething on the mound. He stomped around behind the mound and glared over at Rob Mathews at first base.

Jeb took a few steps toward first and muttered, "No way you guys are beating us today, Mathews . . . you just watch and see."

Rob's face remained a mask at first. *Yeah, we'll see,* Rob thought grimly.

Now, Jeb was back on the mound. He looked in at Trip McHenry . . . *this big punk who transferred in and swung the balance in basketball . . . but it's not going to happen in baseball. Not while I'm pitching,* Jeb thought bitterly.

Jeb stared at Trip . . . hatred spewing. Trip stared back calmly . . . with a twinkle in his eye.

Jeb's head exploded. *This jerk is going down.*

Jeb stood taller, rocked into his windup, and fired a four-seam fast down and in.

Trip was waiting fastball. He saw it coming and timed his swing and launched a moon shot, far down the right field line . . . foul by two feet.

The crowd let out their breath . . . one side in relief and one a groan. Strike one.

Jeb received a new ball and rubbed it up, collecting himself behind the mound.

"Throw that one again, Danielson!!!" rang out from the Hillsdale bleachers.

Jeb stepped back up on the hill. Thought it through. Threw the change.

Trip McHenry swung so hard and early that he knocked himself over. Strike two.

The Pine Bluff crowd was laughing hysterically. The Hillsdale crowd felt that nauseating feeling . . . the one they had felt so often this year . . . *can we ever get a clutch hit?*

Trip McHenry remained calm, even though the crowd was on its feet screaming . . . his teammates yelling out for him to come through . . . while several derogatory remarks could be heard coming from the Pine Bluff dugout.

Jeb Danielson throws. Cutter. Just outside. 1-2 count.

He throws again. Backdoor slider. Just outside. 2-2 count.

Next pitch . . . cutter. Fouled straight back. 2-2 count.

Pitch number six. Backdoor slider. Just missed.

Jeb Danielson goes crazy. Catcher out to head him off before he gets tossed. 3-2 count.

The crowd is now holding its breath on every pitch. From the time Jeb Danielson climbs onto the mound until the ball has been hit, reached the catcher, or been called a ball or strike . . . then a colossal exhalation.

Allison leans over to Emily and squeezes her hand. Emily squeezes back and smiles tightly.

Grandpa Russell, his face taut with excitement, looks at her and smiles.

"You gotta' a good feeling?" Allison yells.

He nods.

"Trip's going to do it," he yells back. "Guaranteed! He's going to do something special!"

Jeb Danielson throws the change. Trip way out in front . . . swinging too hard . . . just gets a piece and trickles it foul up the first base line.

Jeb Danielson again ready . . . winds . . . and throws the change again.

This time . . . Trip guessed right. He waited . . . waited . . . and kept his weight back . . . springing at the perfect moment.

The ball exploded off Trip's bat, and Jeb's head spun around so fast he lost his cap.

At first base, Rob instantly held his arms straight up in the air and slowly started trotting toward second base as he admired the most majestic grand slam he had ever seen.

Trip felt ball meet bat and immediately felt that special feeling. *This one is gone!*

He completed his swing, stood and watched as the ball climbed high and far . . . and watched as Pine Bluff's center-fielder stopped running as the ball soared far over the fence. Only then did Trip leave the box, and he started at a good clip . . . but with his eyes turned to Jeb Danielson near the pitcher's mound . . . glove over his face in despair.

Trip watched Jeb until he had rounded 3rd and saw the team waiting for him at the plate. When he reached home, he was mobbed and hugged by anyone that could get close.

Rob saw pure jubilation in the stands as Hillsdale fans were dancing, cheering, hugging, and kissing . . . it was pandemonium everywhere.

Except in Coach Dave Wilson's mind . . . as he turned to Hulk Thomas.

"Hulk . . . go get loose."

CHAPTER 52
MAY-SOPHOMORE YEAR

C*OACH* Wilson faced one of those decisions that gave coaches premature gray hair.

My pitcher has a perfect game going. Has been dominant. But I have maybe the toughest pitcher in the league to hit right now . . . rested and ready. It's 4-0. Do I make the change? Do I make it to start the inning so Hulk doesn't have to work out of a jam? How do I take Rob out? He'd probably shut them down again . . . maybe with a perfect game!

Coach Wilson pondered that as Bruce Smithers, Toby Tyler, and Matt Bryant hit against a Pine Bluff reliever. They battled but ultimately went down 1-2-3, giving him little time to decide.

After the third out, Coach Wilson sought out Rob and looked at him intently . . . both silent.

"Put Hulk in, Coach," Rob finally said. "I'm tired . . . Hulk is fresh . . . I think he blows them away."

"Whew," Coach Wilson exhaled. "I wasn't sure how to tell you . . . under the circumstances . . ."

"Team first," Rob replied. "Am I at short?"

***

***R**OB* was at short . . . and Hulk Thomas was pitching. As Hulk lumbered in from the bullpen the Pine Bluff PA announcer was saying, "Now pitching for Hillsdale . . . Tubby Thomas."

Rob and Trip winced when they heard that, and Rob trotted toward Hulk on the mound.

"I'm glad they said that," Hulk said, knowing the reason for the visit. "It will just make this so much sweeter."

In the stands, the crowd was uncertain.

"Why are they taking Rob out of pitching?" Allison asked in confusion.

"Not sure," Grandpa Russell said. "Not sure . . . Coach has to know he's got a perfect game going."

"A perfect game?" Allison asked.

"Yes," Grandpa Russell explained. "Rob hadn't allowed a baserunner . . . that's extremely rare . . . you can't talk about them until they're done . . . bad luck . . . interesting he isn't letting Rob try to complete that . . . but . . . I saw Rob and Coach talking . . . and Hulk's his closer . . . I'll be sure to ask Coach later and let you know his thinking . . . if we hold on and win. If not . . . I don't know anyone who will talk to Dave."

Emily grimaced as she listened to her Dad.

The first batter was Pine Bluff's leadoff hitter.

Strike one, strike two, strike three. Cutter. Four-seamer. Cutter.

Now, it was Clem Danielson, and Hulk wore a tight smile on his face.

First pitch. Cutter. Outside corner at the knees. Strike one.

Pitch two. Four-seamer, at the letters inside. Strike Two.

Clem Danielson looked out at Hulk and gritted his teeth.

"Come on, Tubby, let's see your best fastball . . . you can't get me."

Hulk looked in, and got the sign he wanted from Bruce Smithers . . . and threw the most perfect changeup on the planet.

Called strike three!

Clem was mesmerized . . . not expecting the change at all, and he watched it drop on the outside corner at the knees. He heard the umpire ring him up and shouted in protest, getting face-to-face with the umpire, who finally gave him the heave-ho from the game.

Pine Bluff's head coach was face-to-face with the ump, and before too long, he was ejected. The crowd was getting ugly on the Pine Bluff side, calling names at the umpires while the Pirates on the field watched in delight . . . especially Hulk Thomas.

But things were not over. Not only did Hillsdale need one more out to make the Sectionals . . . there was the little matter of the perfect game. And, knowing who stood in his way . . . well, Hulk would not want it any other way.

Jeb Danielson, his lips curled into a treacherous scowl, strode to the plate with just one thing in mind. *Get a hit off Tubby Thomas and at least ruin the perfect game!*

Jeb dug in, snarling out to Hulk, "Come on, Tubby . . . it's my time to hit! Come on . . . Tubbbby . . . bring it!"

First pitch. Changeup. Perfect position. Called strike one.

Jeb growled.

Pitch two. Changeup. Perfect position. Called strike two.

Now, Jeb was livid. *No way he is going to get me . . . he's going to throw the heater. Come on, Tubby, bring it!*

Pitch three. Changeup. Down and away. Out of the strike zone. But . . . swinging strike three!

Jeb Danielson had geared up for a fastball and swung weakly, chasing the change, and disgustedly threw his bat toward the dugout and stomped immediately out of the park.

Hillsdale exploded.

Initially, the team mobbed Hulk Thomas. Rob reached Hulk first and leaped into a giant bear hug. Trip was next, and then the rest of the team.

Then the crowd, spilling out of the stands, reached the field and mobbed the team. Parents, teachers, friends, and family met in the center of the diamond and started dancing, hugging, and kissing.

Rob spotted his Mom and raced over to get a hug. Lisa Cruz was next . . . since she was standing next to Emily . . . and Rob enjoyed his first hug from Lisa. Then . . . Allison . . . an awkward pause . . . and then a big hug . . . and that electric feeling hit Rob again.

Weird. What is that about? Rob asked himself.

The party continued for 15 minutes . . . until Coach Wilson corralled his squad for a talk . . . because the season wasn't over . . . the Sectionals were next.

After the talk and a rambunctious bus ride home, the party started anew in the school parking lot and morphed its way downtown to the park. It was a beautiful spring evening, and the town was out in force to celebrate.

Rob found Trip downtown and pulled him aside . . . alone for the first time since the end of the game.

"Man, you sure came up big," Rob enthused. "I think I need to start calling you "Wonder Boy!"

"Oh, man, no way . . . you were perfect through six," Trip replied. "You're still "Wonder Boy" . . . but maybe we should change it to "Wonder Man!"

They laughed together.

"Hey, how was that . . . getting pulled with a perfecto going?" Trip asked.

"I don't know," Rob answered frankly. "I saw Hulk warming up and I knew it might be the right move . . . but a chance at perfection . . . but you know what . . . I felt like I was a little tired . . . and Hulk . . . he deserved it . . . and what a way to go out."

"You got that right," Trip answered.

"Hey, I was going to ask you," Rob said. "Were you getting worried about your comment about not losing to Pine Bluff?"

"Yeah, a little bit," Trip laughed. "I gotta' learn to shut my mouth. One down . . . about 15 to go!!!"

"Have you forgotten the Valley Christian thing?" Rob asked with a smile.

"No, I haven't . . . but I had hopes that you had," Trip laughed.

"Not a chance," Rob said. "And . . . not a chance Tony Russo has forgotten either!"

"Yeah, I gotta learn to keep my big mouth shut," Trip said sheepishly.

CHAPTER 53
MAY-SOPHOMORE YEAR

ROB woke from a deep sleep to the sounds of Trip McHenry stirring in the bedroom next door. Trip had spent the night . . . because this morning, both boys were heading off to the DMV with Grandpa Russell for their driving tests.

Rob felt that familiar lump in his throat and the butterflies in his stomach, which were signs it was "Big Game" day. And, this qualified . . . especially with Prom tonight. The last thing he wanted to do was fail his test and then have to explain it to kids all night at Prom. *Ugh*, Rob thought. *Why had I let Trip talk me into this . . . Prom . . . I should have said no!*

He met Trip with a smile and a head bob at the top of the stairs, and they both sauntered downstairs and into the kitchen. They were welcomed by Emily, and Grandma and Grandpa Russell . . . and by the huge headline on the front page of the *Hillsdale Express*.

PERFECTION! PINE BLUFF BOUNCED FROM PLAYOFFS BY PIRATES

MATHEWS, THOMAS PERFECT-McHENRY GRAND SLAM KEYS WIN

"Wow!" Rob said, spotting the headline immediately. "Front page! That's pretty impressive!"

"So were you two," Grandpa Russell said with pride. "You guys were terrific! Just like you'll be at the DMV . . . in about an hour . . . we need to get a move on! You guys ready to roll?"

"The "Old Grump" have anything good to say this morning?" Rob asked. "Bet he liked the game."

"He did . . . good stuff in his column," Grandpa Russell replied. "I'll read it to you later . . . after you've passed your tests! Right now . . . we need to hit the road!"

"I packed you guys a breakfast to go," Emily said with a concerned smile. "You sure you don't want me to go with you?"

"No, Mom, thanks," Rob said. "We talked about this . . . Trip and I both agree . . . having just Grandpa there will be better. We'll be a lot less nervous that way . . . if you and Aunt Barb are there . . . well, you know."

"I know, I know," Emily said with a smile. "You do your best . . . both of you . . . if you do that, you'll pass. Call me the minute you're done."

"Will do, Mom," Rob said as he gave her a quick hug and grabbed the Breakfast Burritos she had made.

"You, too, Trip," Emily said, moving to give him a quick hug. "Good luck!"

"It's in the bag . . . guaranteed," Trip answered. He gave Rob a quick look. "Geez, I really need to keep my mouth shut."

They laughed and went out the door with a proud Grandpa Russell leading the way.

A little over an hour later, Rob and Trip had completed their written tests and stood sweating bullets in line to get them assessed.

Rob was first, and he stood staring down at the DMV employee, checking his answers. One wrong, two wrong.

Oh, geez, Rob wailed inside. *NO! I can't fail this test!*

Down the questions they went, correct, correct, correct, wrong answer, correct, correct . . . until finally the DMV lady looked up and smiled at him.

"Congratulations, young man," the lady said. "One down, one to go. Take this over to the line over there . . . someone will take you out for your driving test."

Rob grinned broadly, thanked the lady, and turned to give Trip . . . and then Grandpa Russell a relieved thumbs up. *Now, for the hard part,* Rob thought.

Grandpa Russell shook his hand and wished him luck.

Rob went to the next counter, keeping a close eye on Trip, nervous for his friend.

Trip's head was hunched over, carefully watching the lady, and then he straightened up, and Rob could see him relax. He turned quickly and flashed a relieved grin at Rob . . . just as the man assigned to do Rob's driving portion of the test arrived.

Here we go, Rob gulped.

Trip and Grandpa Russell waited while Rob went out to drive . . . five minutes . . . ten minutes . . . 15 minutes . . . until they both saw Rob pulling into the DMV parking lot through the large window.

They could see the man pointing at his clipboard, talking to Rob while still seated in the car. Rob was nodding and his head was down. They started to climb out of the car. Rob stood up, turned around . . . and cracked a huge smile when he saw Grandpa Russell and Trip in the window.

One down, one to go, Grandpa Russell thought.

Now, it was Trip's turn . . . and while Rob had his photo taken and received his temporary license, Grandpa Russell watched nervously at the window.

Please let him pass, Grandpa Russell thought. *Please let him pass, too!*

Grandpa Russell felt Rob at his elbow.

"No sign of him yet?" Rob asked.

Grandpa Russell shook his head.

Boy, Grandpa looks nervous, Rob realized. *I guess he really cares about us . . . he really wants us to succeed. Well . . . he did put a lot of time and effort into teaching us.*

The car pulled into sight. Same routine. Going over the clipboard. Trip nods . . . listens . . . nods some more . . . listens again . . . not looking happy . . . gets out of the car. Stone-faced.

Grandpa Russell and Rob glance at each other.

"Oh no," Rob said immediately.

"Oh, no!" Grandpa Russell echoed.

Together they watched Trip retrieve the car keys and head toward the doors slowly, head down, somber. He went out of sight momentarily and then came through the doors and into the building . . . with a massive grin on his face.

Rob and Grandpa Russell both heaved a sigh of relief. Rob gave Trip a hard high-five, and Grandpa Russell gave him a huge bear hug.

"Don't do that again," Grandpa Russell said roughly. "You almost gave me a heart attack!"

CHAPTER 54
MAY-SOPHOMORE YEAR

ONE down, two to go, Rob thought after he had celebrated quickly with his Mom and Grandma. *Next comes dancing lessons with Allison . . . and then the Prom. What a day!*

Rob walked nervously to Allison's for his 2:00 dance lesson and knocked on the door. Allison swung the door open and was absolutely glowing.

Wow! Rob thought. *What is different? Same goofy glasses. Same tin grin. Same straight black hair hanging down to the middle of her back. Same great smile! What's different?*

Allison beamed at Rob, and he smiled back. They went through the door and into the living room, where Allison had moved furniture aside to create a small dance floor.

"Congratulations on your driving test!" Allison said once the door was closed.

Allison moved closer as if to hug him . . . but she stopped short . . . unsure of herself.

It's funny, Rob thought quickly. *Girls are always hugging their guy friends . . . I see it all the time. I wonder why Allison and I never hug?*

"How did you . . . ?" Rob began. "Oh, yeah . . . you have a direct pipeline through my Mom."

Allison laughed.

"She was so excited for you," Allison said. "She had to tell someone!"

"And that, of course, had to be you," Rob said with a soft chuckle.

"Who else?" Allison laughed again. "And, congrats on yesterday's game . . . I didn't get to see you after the game . . . it was so crowded . . . and I didn't want to bother you downtown last night . . . you know . . . intrude on the big *"spooorts"* heroes!"

"Allison, you wouldn't be a bother or be intruding," Rob said sincerely. "You're one of the gang . . . you should have joined us."

Allison winced at being "one of the gang" but said, "I'm sure I'll have another chance. You guys aren't done winning big games."

"I hope you're right," Rob smiled.

"So, let's get down to dancing," Allison grinned.

Rob groaned. *I guess that's what I'm here for.*

"Let's start with fast dancing," Allison said firmly but with a smile. "That's where you need the most work!"

"Fast dancing! I don't want to have to fast dance," Rob complained.

"You are going to the Prom . . . with juniors and seniors . . . they are going to expect you to be mature enough to fast dance," Allison said lightly. "Besides, I know Lisa loves to dance."

What did I get myself into? Rob wondered.

"I don't know how to fast dance," Rob protested. "I look ridiculous when I fast dance."

"No one is looking at you when you fast dance," Allison replied.

"Yeah . . . because I don't fast dance . . . if I'm out there, they will be laughing at me," Rob said.

"No one watches other people dance . . . or makes fun of them," Allison said, trying to calm his fears. "People don't do that."

"They do, too," Rob retorted. "I know . . . because my friends and I stand on the side and laugh at all the lousy dancers at every dance."

Allison was surprised.

"Really?" Allison asked skeptically. "You guys laugh at people for bad dancing?"

"Absolutely," Rob said, hoping he had won this argument. "Every dance."

"Well, shame on you," Allison said in mock horror. "I guess you'll just have to get used to people laughing at you . . . unless you learn what I teach today . . ."

Rob just stared at her . . . and he knew that look.

"OK, OK, what do I do?" Rob asked with a sigh of resignation.

"Well, really . . . you have it lucky," Allison said with a smile. "You're such a hot shot athlete . . . you just have to stand out there and basically let the girl dance around you."

"Well, that doesn't sound so hard," Rob replied. "Or, so funny looking."

"Right . . . it's not," Allison said. "Let me put on some songs, and I'll show you."

CHAPTER 55
MAY-SOPHOMORE YEAR

FOR the next half hour, Allison tried to get Rob to loosen up and relax, but it was tough going.

"How can such a good athlete not be able to move his arms and legs a little bit to music?" Allison finally asked. "You do unbelievable things with your body every day on the field or the court. Just relax and let them dangle. Move your feet just a little and sway from side to side . . . there you go . . . that's it."

"This is just too hard for me . . . I have no clue what to do," Rob said, losing hope. "I don't think this is helping!"

"No, no . . . that last little bit was fine," Allison coached. "Do that again for one more song, and we'll call it good."

The song came on, and Rob did his thing . . . and Allison worked to suppress a smile. *He's so cute,* she thought. *He is trying so hard . . . but he is pretty bad! I can't tell him that, though . . . or Lisa will never get him on the dance floor!*

"There . . . that's great," Allison said, stretching the truth a little. "Just do that tonight with Lisa . . . and you'll be great!"

"OK, if you think that's OK, I'll go with it," Rob answered unenthusiastically.

"You'll be great!" Allison said, trying to boost his confidence. "Now, let me put on a couple of slow dances."

This was the moment, unbeknownst to the other, that the two of them had been both waiting for . . . and dreading.

The music started, and Allison came toward Rob with her arms outstretched, and a reassuring smile plastered on her face.

Rob moved toward her, and they bumped awkwardly. Rob reacted swiftly, changed positions, and pulled her closer into a halfway decent dancing position, apologizing all the way.

When he got Allison securely in his arms, Rob felt that same electric charge pulse through his body, and it caused him to jerk back slightly.

"Don't be nervous," Allison soothed. "Just sway slowly to the music and move your feet a little . . . like this."

Allison showed Rob a few dance steps, and the two nestled closer together, becoming more comfortable with the other's position.

What am I feeling? Rob wondered frantically. *Allison feels so good . . . smells so good . . . I don't want this to end.*

At the same time, Allison was thinking much the same. *Oh, please don't let this stop. I'm so glad I picked two long, slow songs to play.*

They drifted around the floor . . . both silent and lost in their thoughts. The first song ended, and they held each other until the second song started and then resumed their slow rocking across the floor.

This feels like it did with Stephanie . . . and Carly . . . and when Dee Dee kissed me last year, Rob thought. His head was swirling, and he felt off balance. *I hope she doesn't ask me anything . . . I'd probably do anything for her right now.*

Allison's head was spinning, too. *I have dreamed about doing this for so long . . . since Homecoming freshman year. And here I am. Why didn't I put three slow songs in the queue? Or, four songs . . . or five??!!*

The song was winding down . . . they both knew it . . . and they nestled a little closer . . . neither really wanting the song to end.

This cannot be happening, Rob thought. *Me and Allison? She is so goofy looking! But really . . . does that matter? What do I care what she looks like? She makes me happy . . . she makes me laugh . . . she is so wonderful to me . . . but . . . she's such a geek . . . and I'm such a jerk!*

Slow down, song, Allison prayed. *I want this to last a little longer . . . a lot longer. But what do I say now . . . he's going to Prom with Lisa . . . ? I can't wreck that. Be smart . . . be nice. Don't stop . . . please don't let this song end.*

Then it was over.

After the music stopped, they remained in each other's arms for a long minute. Her head was on his shoulder, and their arms were locked tight. She sighed deeply. So did he. She pushed him away softly, and their eyes met. They gazed at each other and then . . .

"Well," Allison said, sharply backing away from Rob. "I think you've got the slow dancing down . . . Lisa will love that!"

That snapped Rob back to reality. *Lisa? Oh, yeah. Lisa. The Prom. Lisa? Allison? What is going on? I am just so completely confused right now!*

"Oh, you think so," Rob stammered, backing away a bit further.

"Yep," Allison said quickly. "I think you've got it. You're ready to dazzle the crowd and your date! Tonight, you earn that "Wonder Boy" nickname! You'll show everyone you've got the moves on the dance floor, too!"

With that, the spell was broken, and things were back to normal.

"You've got to get going, "Wonder Boy," Allison said brightly. "You've got to get shined up for your big date . . . and that might take a while. Got someone to help you with your Tux?"

"Very funny, Ally!" Rob said.

Ally . . . Ally . . . I love it when he calls me Ally! Allison thought with joy.

"I wore a Tux last year for Prom," Rob said proudly.

Rob paused and then added, "My Mom helped me get it on right . . . it's tough."

Allison howled with laughter, and after a second, Rob did, too.

"I'd like to see you get a Tux on by yourself!" Rob exclaimed lightly.

"Oh, get out of here . . . and get ready," Allison insisted. "You don't want to be late."

"No, no, I don't," Rob said as he opened the door and stepped through, shutting the door behind him.

Oh, Rob, don't go! Allison thought. *No . . . no, I know you have to go . . . but please don't like Lisa too much.*

There was a light tap at the door, and Allison raced to open it.

"Hey, Ally . . . I almost forgot . . . thanks a bunch for the dancing lessons," Rob said with a shy smile. "I just don't know what I'd do without you, Ally! You're the best!"

Ally . . . Ally . . . I love it when he calls me Ally!

CHAPTER 56
MAY-SOPHOMORE YEAR

*A*FTER almost an hour of picture taking, parents gawking and saying how wonderful everyone looked, Rob, Lisa, Trip, and Jillian finally said their goodbyes. They hopped in their cars, which were parked in the street in front of Jillian's house. Lisa and Rob were in Lisa's VW Bug, and Jillian was driving Trip to dinner and the Prom in her folk's car.

The whirlwind of photos and extra people had left Rob unable to focus on anything, and as Lisa started the car and drove away, he let out a long sigh and really looked at Lisa for the first time that day.

She is gorgeous, Rob thought, gazing at her with fresh eyes. *She's wearing makeup . . . and she looks . . . great. What can I say? I'm still a jerk! Lisa is hot! Allison will kill me for thinking that! But at least I know her . . . and like her!*

Lisa felt Rob's eyes on her and turned to catch him staring at her.

"What?" she asked with a halting laugh.

"What?" she repeated when he just sat there.

"I just . . . just," Rob sputtered. "You just look great, Lisa!"

"Yeah, yeah," Lisa laughed. "It's the makeup . . . what a pain."

"Well, it's . . . you . . . look good," Rob stammered.

"Well, thanks, Rob," Lisa said sincerely. "You clean up pretty well yourself."

Quickly both cars reached the restaurant, and the foursome piled out and headed in to see if they could act like adults in a fancy restaurant. They couldn't.

But they did a pretty good job.

Jillian and Trip were really just friends . . . *I think Trip may want to be more than friends,* Rob thought. *Jillian is really hot!*

Being just friends . . . kind of like Lisa and Rob were just friends, made for light conversation and plenty of laughs.

Rob was obviously the most awkward in mixed company, but the other three's demeanor soon made him feel comfortable, and quickly the two couples were bantering back and forth like old married couples.

The laughter came easy and was genuine, and Rob felt drawn more and more to Lisa's perky personality. Since all of them were athletes, the conversation started there but branched out naturally to other things.

When dinner was over and it was time to be alone with Lisa again, Rob thought nothing of it. *This is nothing like last year with Dee Dee . . . or like dating Stephanie or Carly. This is pretty easy,* Rob realized.

When they arrived at the Prom, a fashionable 15 minutes late, the dancing had already started, and almost everybody had arrived.

The first person they ran into was Bruce Smithers . . . who rushed over when he saw them come in . . . looking like he had something important to say.

"Hey, guys," Bruce said, acknowledging their whole group. "Did you hear the news?" Bruce asked, excitement in his eyes.

"News . . . what news?" Trip asked.

"Seedings for Sectionals are in," Bruce replied with a twinkle in his eyes.

"Who do we open up with?" Rob asked with interest.

"We got seeded #9 . . . so we play #8 in the first round on Wednesday," Bruce said.

"Whose #8?" Trip demanded.

"Cooley," Bruce answered.

Rob and Trip were stunned.

"I . . . I didn't expect them to be so low," Rob said slowly, digesting the news.

"Me, either," said Bruce.

"Cooley," Trip echoed. "I like it . . . they're not going to beat us three times in one season! This is perfect!"

"It is perfect," Rob agreed, his mind racing ahead. "And, when we win, we get #1 . . . I'm going to guess Valley Christian . . ."

"Good guess!" Bruce laughed.

Rob looked at Trip, who had a sheepish grin on his face.

"I know . . . Tony Russo . . . good memory . . . I just gotta' remember to keep my mouth shut!" Trip said with a laugh.

CHAPTER 57
MAY-SOPHOMORE YEAR

*T*HE news traveled quickly through the Prom, and for a short while, there was a baseball buzz in the building. But soon, the girls at the Prom tired of it, and the conversations turned to other things, and the dance floor got more crowded.

Rob was enjoying Lisa's company . . . and that of all his older friends in attendance . . . some of whom had invited sophomores and freshmen as dates.

Dee Dee Baker greeted him with a happy kiss, and Rob chatted with her boyfriend, Don Harbin, for a while. Stephanie Miller was there with Phil Boyer, and she snagged Rob for the first slow dance of the night . . . as Lisa and Phil had coincidently gone to the restrooms just before the slow dance began.

Rob noticed that the electric surge when he held Stephanie in his arms to dance was still there . . . but was not nearly as strong. She was chattering away, and Rob just enjoyed holding her again . . . *oh, I remember her perfume . . . but something is missing . . . it's not like it was when we dated. And nothing like what I felt this afternoon with Allison!*

The song ended, their dates returned, and Rob returned to the dance floor again with Lisa for some fast dances. Rob basically stood in one place and let Lisa dance beautifully around him. *I can't believe it,* Rob thought, watching her . . . *she is hot! And she's here with me!*

He saw Carly Neel across the room, and she looked away quickly, running her hands up the arm of her senior class date. *Dodged a bullet there. Thanks, Trip!* Rob mused.

A half a dozen fast songs later . . . a slow dance . . . and Rob breathed a sigh of relief and held his hand out to Lisa.

"Shall we?" Rob asked with exaggerated formality.

"Why, yes, thank you, sir," Lisa giggled.

They moved to the floor, Rob pulled her close, and they settled in.

Nothing.

No surge . . . no nothing. What's wrong here? Rob wondered frantically. *I like Lisa. A lot. Where is the spark? What's going on?*

They continued to dance . . . and it was nice. They spoke quietly to each other while they danced . . . laughing . . . making sly jokes about other kids . . . acting just like they did in Science every day. *It's fun . . . but something's missing,* Rob realized.

The band took their last break when the dance ended, and the kids gravitated to the food and drink table until the band returned.

Maybe I'll feel it the next slow dance, Rob hoped.

Nope. Nothing.

The last dance . . . that'll do it, Rob hoped again.

Looking at the clock, Rob knew the next song would be the last dance . . . *the last slow dance,* he thought as Lisa laughed at one of Trip's jokes. *What is wrong here? I really, really like Lisa. She is funny, she is smart, she is an athlete . . . she is HOTTT! Why don't I feel that spark? What is wrong with me?*

The current song ended, and with it came the formal announcement of the last song . . . and the strains of a long, love ballad started up. Rob turned to Lisa, took her hand, and she followed him to the dance floor.

He smiled at her as he turned to gather her to him, and she smiled back at him warmly.

"This has been so much fun, Rob. Thank you so much for saying yes and coming tonight," Lisa smiled brightly at him before nestling in close.

Nothing. Nada. Zilch. *What is wrong with you? You like this girl a lot. What is wrong with you? Is it Allison?*

It hit Rob like a ton of bricks. *It's Allison,* he realized. *I want to be with Allison Pierce!!!! Wait! What???!!! Calm down. Enjoy this dance with Lisa. She is so nice. So right for you. But . . . Allison . . . all I can think of is Allison.*

Lisa pulled away from Rob and looked at him funny.

"You OK, Rob?" she asked.

"Yeah, yeah," Rob mumbled, pulling her closer. "I'm fine." *Fine??? You're a basket case,* Rob thought. *I can't be going through this during Sectionals. Put it out of your mind. No girls until after Sectionals . . . but how do I tell Lisa about this? She is so great. Aw, geez . . . I hate dating!*

***

A short 30 minutes later, Lisa pulled her car onto a dark side street, stopped, and turned to face Rob.

"Rob, I know you have a curfew . . . but this won't take long," Lisa said, looking at him soulfully.

She reached over and touched his face lightly, looked deeply into his eyes, and pulled his face to kiss him softly.

Nothing. Nada. Zilch.

Lisa pulled away from the kiss and looked at Rob with a warm smile.

"Rob . . . I'm so sorry," Lisa began. "I like you so, sooo much . . . you are so fun . . . and so nice . . . but . . . but there's just no spark for us as boyfriend and girlfriend."

Rob's face flooded with relief.

"Oh, geez, Lisa . . . do you feel it, too?" Rob replied.

"You, too," Lisa said with immense relief. "Oh, Rob . . . you don't know how happy that makes me. The last thing I would ever want to do is hurt you . . . you are really a special guy . . . and I really want us to stay friends . . . I don't want that to change . . . but dancing with you . . . kissing you . . . it was like doing that with my brother!"

Rob didn't know which to feel first . . . the pain of Lisa's rejection . . . or the joy of knowing they both felt the same way.

"Oh, Lisa . . . I feel the same way . . . not about kissing a brother . . . aw, you know what I mean," Rob laughed.

They both laughed and sighed with relief.

"I had so much fun tonight, Lisa," Rob recovered. "I really did . . . but I just didn't get the couple spark either . . . not that I really know what that is . . ."

"You are a real catch, Rob Mathews . . . if you haven't already been caught," Lisa said with a wink. "I really don't want anything to change between us, Rob . . . you're a great friend, and I don't want to lose that. Do you promise?"

"Promise," Rob answered sincerely.

"Well, then I better get you home . . . before your Mom calls the cops on me," Lisa grinned.

They both laughed hard, and five minutes later, they gave each other a big hug, a kiss on the cheek, and said goodnight.

Allison? Allison Pierce? Really? Rob thought. *After Sectionals, Rob . . . after Sectionals.*

CHAPTER 58
MAY-SOPHOMORE YEAR

"*Oh*, hi, Mom," Rob said softly as he spotted his Mom snuggled up on the couch.

"Hi, Rob!" Emily replied brightly while she glanced at the clock. "Right on time, as usual."

"Yeah . . . don't want to have to be here a minute longer than I have to be," Rob retorted sarcastically, and Emily joined in his laughter.

"Soooo, how was Prom?" Emily asked.

"It was great," Rob answered excitedly. "Lisa was great . . . really fun . . . dinner with Trip and Jillian was great, too . . . we laughed so hard."

Emily smiled, pleased that Rob was so excited.

"And, the dancing part . . . ?" Emily prompted.

"That was OK, too," Rob answered. "I even fast danced about ten times . . . slow danced with Stephanie once . . . and with Lisa three or four times."

"So, you and Lisa hit it off?" Emily asked, thinking, *this is going to be hard on Allison.*

"Yeah, she is hilarious . . . and . . . well, you saw her . . . she is hot . . . but she was just really fun to be with," Rob said enthusiastically.

"Well . . . does that mean you guys are . . . what do you call it . . . talking . . . or dating . . . hanging out . . . or what?" Emily quizzed.

"Well," Rob began. "Funny thing there . . . after she kissed me . . ."

"Whoa . . . slow down," Emily laughed. "She kissed you? When? Where?"

"On the way home . . . on the mouth?" Rob replied.

Emily cracked up.

"Not where on your face . . . where?" Emily laughed.

"Oh, a few blocks away . . . dark, quiet street," Rob teased.

"And, what's funny about that?" Emily persisted.

"Well, I had been feeling it earlier . . . and I think she had, too," Rob explained. "And she wanted to test it by kissing me."

"Test what?" Emily asked in confusion.

"Whether there was any spark," Rob said.

"And . . ." Emily prompted again.

"Nothing. Nada. Zilch," Rob laughed.

Emily cracked up again.

"But I thought you told me you both had a great time?" Emily asked, now even more confused.

"We did . . . I really like her, Mom . . . and I think she really likes me . . . but as friends," Rob explained. "She said kissing me was like kissing her brother!"

"Ouch!" Emily said.

"No . . . it was fine, Mom . . . because . . . well, I noticed it when we were dancing . . . no spark like there was with Stephanie or Carly . . . or . . ." Rob trailed off.

"Or?" Emily asked.

"Well," Rob said with embarrassment, "with Allison . . ."

"Allison?" Emily said in shock.

"Yeah . . . weird, huh?!" Rob replied.

"Are you going to tell Allison?" Emily asked with growing concern.

"No . . . not right away," Rob said slowly. "I've got Sectionals coming up . . . I don't want to deal with girl stuff right now. But maybe after . . . and don't tell Allison, please!"

"I won't . . . but I'm very impressed, Rob," Emily said. "What changed your mind?"

"You know that big blow-up at school about her not dating me if she got hot . . . it made me start thinking about what's important," Rob confessed. "I'm happiest when I'm around Allison . . . you know . . . with girls . . . except for you, of course, Mom."

"Nice try," Emily laughed at the last remark. "But you're not doing this because you feel sorry for her, are you?"

"No, Mom," Rob said honestly. "I just can't stop thinking about her."

"Well, you know," Emily smiled, "I have always been a big fan of Allison."

"I know . . . I know . . . Prom Queen in the making," Rob laughed. "Like that will ever happen."

"Oh, don't be so sure it won't," Emily laughed back. "But I'm not talking about that. I'm talking about Allison . . . the person. She's an old soul . . ."

Emily paused and laughed, seeing the confusion on Rob's face.

"She's one of those kids that would have been comfortable growing up in the 1950s or 1960s," Emily explained. "She would have been called old-fashioned even when I went to school. She loves the old movies, old songs . . . listens to the lyrics . . ."

"*You've Got a Friend* . . . by Carole King," Rob threw in.

"Exactly," Emily grinned. "But she also has old-fashioned values already that a lot of kids don't get . . . at least not at this age. She wants a small-town family life . . . just like her folks and grandparents . . . just like Grandma and Grandpa Russell. You know, stay in your hometown forever. That's certainly not for everyone . . . but it will work for Allison. She's a real keeper."

"Well, I don't know about that," Rob said, trying to process the information. "I'm not saying I'm going to marry her or anything! She's just fun . . . and comfortable to be around. And, that spark I feel sometimes . . . I don't know . . . it's crazy."

"You'll figure it out . . . when the time is right," Emily laughed. "And, you're right . . . you're way too young to be thinking about forever!"

I hope this isn't too soon, Emily thought when they both padded off to bed a few minutes later. *I don't want Allison to get hurt . . . or Rob.*

CHAPTER 59
MAY-SOPHOMORE YEAR

THE following day, Rob padded into the kitchen at 9:00 am to find his Mom and Grandparents hovered around the *Hillsdale Express* as usual . . . and a little surprisingly, Trip McHenry was there as well.

"Finally awake, huh?" Trip drawled with a small laugh. "Late night?"

"I'll tell you all about it later," Rob said with a smile.

"I'm here to see if I can hit this morning," Trip continued. "Aunt Barb wants me to drive her down to Sacramento today to shop . . . and I won't be back until "Movie Night.""

Rob nodded.

"Ah, yes . . . you guys are drivers now," Grandpa Russell smiled broadly. "You did a great job yesterday . . . both of you."

"We had a good teacher," Trip piped in.

"That's for sure," Rob echoed.

"Well, now for the most important thing of the day," Grandpa Russell pronounced. "Want to hear what the "Old Grump" has to say about the Sectionals?"

Grandma Russell and Emily rolled their eyes at Grandpa's "most important thing of the day."

"All right, here we go," Grandpa Russell said, ignoring the eye-rolling, as he started to read Dan Mercer's column aloud.

"The Hillsdale Pirates got a tough seed in this year's Sectionals, drawing #9, and a first-round date with their nemesis of the year . . . the Cooley Cougars, and lefthander Seth Gardner. This year, Gardner was especially tough on the Pirates, allowing just one rain-induced unearned run in 14 innings. He's tough."

Rob and Trip both nodded.

"He is tough," Trip said, shaking his head.

"Wait, there's more," Grandpa Russell said.

"As tough as it will be to get by Gardner and the Cooley Cougars . . . the winner gets no prize . . . instead a date with top-seeded Valley Christian . . . at their field in the Quarterfinals."

More head nodding before Grandpa Russell continued reading.

"I have it on good authority that Coach Dave Wilson plans to give the ball to Jose Rivera against Cooley. One could argue that Rob Mathews might be the best choice . . . remember, saving Mathews for Valley Christian does you no good at all if you don't get by Cooley. But Rivera was most impressive against Cooley this year . . . giving up just one earned run in 12 innings of work. It wasn't his fault Hillsdale dropped both league games to Cooley this year . . . the fault lies with the utter ineptitude of the offense to produce in the clutch."

Grandpa Russell paused to let that sink in and finished the article.

"Still, I have to like Hillsdale's chances on Wednesday. It's tough to beat a good team three times in a row . . . and I have to believe that offense will finally solve Seth Gardner and put some runs on the board. Hillsdale wins this one. Valley Christian? Another story for another day. Look for it Saturday morning . . . if Hillsdale gets by Cooley on Wednesday."

"Can't fault his logic," Rob acknowledged begrudgingly. "We have been pitiful against Gardner."

"That's why I'm here so early," trumpeted Trip McHenry. "Ready to get started . . . I hope so . . . because I'm ready, and I need help."

"Let's go," said Rob.

***

"*So*, you're really OK about it," Allison asked Rob as they sat on Allison's front porch waiting for Trip to arrive for "Movie Night."

"Yeah," Rob answered. "Lisa was great all night . . . but neither of us felt that spark . . . you know."

No, I don't know, reflected Allison. *Unless that's what I felt giving you dance lessons!*

"But we're still going to be friends . . . we really had fun last night," Rob added.

"Yeah, that's what Lisa said," Allison replied. "She said it was great fun . . . but just . . ."

"Yeah," Rob laughed. "Just like kissing her brother . . ."

Allison smiled at him, knowing he was OK . . . but that the comment probably hurt a little.

There was a long pause, and both felt an underlying awkwardness . . . a carryover from the dancing lesson . . . and Rob's reluctance to broach the subject of his feelings before Sectionals were over.

"How are your trip plans coming?" Allison asked, finally breaking the silence.

"Great," Rob said. "We're leaving Sunday after school gets out and will be gone three and a half weeks . . . home a few days and off to basketball camp . . . I'm jazzed about summer!"

"Me, too," Allison said with equal enthusiasm.

"When are you heading off to Europe?" Rob asked.

"Still up in the air," Allison said, grinning at her play on words. "We're still not sure . . . we're flying standby . . . remember?"

Rob laughed, finally understanding the joke.

"No idea at all?" Rob asked.

"Well, it will be between ten days and two weeks. We're just not sure," Allison explained.

"You might miss the Sectional Semifinals and Finals!" Rob exclaimed. "How can you do that? Wait . . . what will my Mom and Grandpa Russell do without you in the bleachers?"

What will I do without you in the bleachers? Rob thought.

"I don't know . . . ?" Allison said, trailing off. "I never thought of that . . . I can't miss a Sectional Championship game!"

"I can't imagine you not being there," Rob said, suddenly melancholy.

"Me either," Allison said, looking Rob directly in the eyes.

A long pause as they gazed at each other.

Should I tell her now? Rob wondered. *No, no, I've got too much to worry about already with finals at school and Sectionals. But . . . maybe I should . . .*

"Allison," Rob said, lowering his eyes and then lifting them to meet Allison's eyes.

"Yes . . . ?" Allison replied expectantly.

"HEY, GUYS!!! WHAT'S HAPPENING!!!!"

It was Trip McHenry . . . shattering the moment as he arrived for "Movie Night."

CHAPTER 60
MAY-SOPHOMORE YEAR

WEDNESDAY afternoon. Bus ride to Cooley. Game one of the Sectionals. One and done. Cooley trying to beat Hillsdale for the third time.

Perfect day . . . 80 degrees. Slight breeze. Bleachers packed. Standing room only.

Seth Gardner versus Jose Rivera. Pitcher's duel. Again.

Both pitchers took up right where they left off the last time they faced each other . . . just eight days ago . . . but that one was in Hillsdale.

Today, Cooley was at home, and their boisterous fans were at full force. Seth Gardner was, too.

He set the Pirates down in quickly in the first . . . no problem.

Jose Rivera followed suit.

Again, in the second . . . and the third . . . and the fourth . . . a hit here or there for both teams . . . but no scoring threats . . . no baserunners made it as far and second base.

The crowd was getting anxious. The players were getting tight. Every pitch was huge. Every play . . . every throw . . . every swing. Mouths were dry . . . stomachs were full of knots . . . who was going to cave first?

***

*I*T started with a dink, with two outs in the 5th inning. Seth Gardner was on cruise control, and he let a curve ball to Gavin Ford catch a little too much of the plate, and the speedy right-fielder dinked it into center field just out of the shortstop's reach.

Buck Buckman followed with a seeing-eye ground ball that rolled past a diving third baseman and into left field.

Mark Porter was next, and Gardner, aware that Rob Mathews was next, lost focus and walked Porter on six pitches.

Bases loaded. Two outs. Scoreless game.

The entire crowd standing for one pitch.

Then one side sat down.

Cooley sat down.

Rob Mathews sat them down.

Rob blasted Gardner's first pitch on a line into the left-center field gap, and the base runners were off to the races. Gavin Ford and Buck Buckman scored, and it was 2-0 Hillsdale.

The Hillsdale crowd . . . especially Rob's family . . . and Allison Pierce . . . went bananas!

Before the Hillsdale crowd could quiet down . . . boom . . . another rocket . . . this one off the bat of Trip McHenry . . . a searing line drive down the right field line. Mark Porter walked home from third while Rob Mathews scampered in behind him, and it was 4-0.

A shaken Seth Gardner tried his best to regroup. He got a quick two strikes on Bruce Smithers . . . but on pitch three, Smithers creamed a towering fly ball to dead center field, and the entire crowd watched as it soared over the fence for a two-run homer and a 6-0 Hillsdale lead!

In the stands, it was pandemonium. On the bench, it was all business.

"A long way to go, guys," Coach Wilson reminded his players as they ran out to play defense in the bottom of the 5th.

They were out there for three minutes. Jose Rivera sliced and diced his way through the Cougar lineup, going 1-2-3 on just ten pitches.

Seth Gardner was gone when the Pirates started the 6th, and they immediately pounced on his reliever. Matt Bryant singled, as did Josh Lee. Gavin Ford sacrificed them to second and third . . . and Buck Buckman doubled them home to make it 8-0.

After Mark Porter flew out, Cooley chose to walk Rob Mathews intentionally . . . and Trip McHenry made them pay with a towering three-run homer.

The crowd was absolutely stunned . . . on both sides of the field . . . but one side was in stunned silence . . . while the other side was dancing in the bleachers.

And, just minutes later . . . Jose Rivera induced Cooley's last chance to hit a soft fly ball to Buck Buckman in center, and the game was over after just six innings . . . 11-0 Hillsdale.

The mood in the Hillsdale stands was jubilation. On the bench . . . not so much. They were, of course, happy to have exorcized the Cooley demon . . . but they knew who was next on the agenda . . . the Valley Christian Knights.

CHAPTER 61
MAY-SOPHOMORE YEAR

"**LOOK** who's here," Tony Russo roared, walking into Pop's Diner Thursday night.

Sitting in a booth were Rob, Trip, Buck, and Hulk . . . and they all groaned in unison as Tony approached with his ever-present entourage.

"What do you want, Tony?" Rob asked, hoping to get rid of him as quickly as possible.

"Oh, I just wanted to congratulate you guys on the big win," Tony said smoothly. "Never figured you guys would beat Cooley . . . figured you'd lose on purpose just to avoid us!"

Silence.

"Yeah, you think Gardner's good," Tony said. "Wait until you see our ace . . . Baker's going to eat you guys alive."

Silence.

"I hear you're the ace for Hillsdale, Mathews . . . that's going to be fun . . . for us," Tony jabbed.

Silence.

"What's the matter with you guys," Tony said as he and his group laughed loudly. "You too afraid to even talk to us? I bet you're not too afraid to talk to us . . . are you, McHenry?"

Silence.

"Yeah, you weren't too afraid a while ago . . . I think I remember," Tony continued. "I think I remember you saying Hillsdale would never lose to Valley Christian again at anything . . . do you remember that, McHenry? You know anything includes baseball, right?"

Silence.

Except for the cackling of the Valley Christian crowd.

"Well, we'll burst that little bubble on Saturday for good," Tony added. "Then we'll see how much you want to open your big mouth."

Silence.

"We'll see you on Saturday, losers . . . and we'll be sure to celebrate hard in front of you," Tony laughed as he and his group turned and piled into a booth on the other side of Pop's.

All eyes at the table turned on Trip.

Trip shrugged sheepishly and softly chuckled.

"Good thing Tony didn't remember what you said," Rob finally said.

Trip led the loud laughter at the table.

"Yeah . . . I really don't like that guy . . . and . . . I think I need help keeping my mouth shut," Trip answered.

"We'll all pitch in to help you do that," Buck laughed.

"Yeah, Trip . . . we've all heard that before," Rob said playfully. "But it might be a good idea . . ."

CHAPTER 62

MAY-SOPHOMORE YEAR

*S*ATURDAY morning, Rob awoke to butterflies. *Funny, I don't remember these for the Cooley game . . . but this is Valley Christian . . . and I can feel it. Valley Christian games are definitely feeling like Pine Bluff games now!*

First pitch was scheduled for 1:00 pm, so the bus was leaving Hillsdale High at 11:00 am. Rob was up early, showered and ready to roll, and strolled into the kitchen to find the usual suspects . . . his Mom and Grandparents . . . and Grandpa Russell was holding up the *Hillsdale Express*.

"Hi, Rob," Grandpa Russell said as he walked in and sat down.

"Ready to hear what Dan Mercer has to say this morning?" Grandpa Russell asked excitedly.

"You do love reading the paper out loud, don't you, Dad," Emily laughed.

"Sometimes, I think he just likes to hear the sound of his own voice," Grandma Russell chuckled.

"Never you mind, Flo," Grandpa Russell chided his wife.

"Ahem," Grandpa Russell cleared his throat . . . something he almost always did before reading out loud.

"One of the strangest baseball seasons in my recollection is nearing an end for the Hillsdale Pirates. Will it be this afternoon against heavily favored Valley Christian . . . or can the Pirates pull off a mini-miracle and extend their season until at least next Wednesday? The Pirates have seemed an elite team at times this year . . . but those games . . . like the one against Braxton . . . were tantalizing . . . but in the end, losses. They beat Pine Bluff twice! They lost to Cooley twice! Both times in one-run losses in gut-wrenching style . . . scoring only one run in two games! And then . . . they trounce Cooley in the Sectionals with an offensive explosion of 11 runs in two innings!"

Grandpa Russell paused to be sure his audience was paying attention.

"Today, we'll see Rob Mathews on the mound, fresh off a perfect six-inning stint against Pine Bluff. Hulk Thomas will be ready to close . . . if needed . . . but which Hillsdale offense is going to show up? The one that struggled with their clutch hitting for much of the year, missing chance after chance to get that big hit . . . score that big run . . . win that big game. Or, the one that showed up against Cooley Wednesday afternoon?"

"Good question . . ." Grandpa Russell said.

"Wish I had an answer," Rob grunted.

"They might not need to score a bunch, with Mathews and Thomas . . . and I imagine Jose Rivera available . . . but they will have to score at least one . . . two . . . maybe three to beat Valley Christian," Grandpa Russell continued reading. "Can they do it?"

"What do you think the "Old Grump" says, Rob?" Grandpa Russell teased.

Rob made a show of thinking deeply and finally said, "One team will win . . . and the other will lose?"

Emily and Grandma Russell were amused . . . Grandpa Russell . . . not so much.

"I'm going out on a limb here," Grandpa Russell read, "but against all odds, heavy odds for you betting folks out there . . . I'm calling for a Hillsdale upset win today over Valley Christian. Look for Rob Mathews, Buck Buckman, Trip McHenry, and Hulk Thomas to be the keys today. You read it here first!"

CHAPTER 63
MAY-SOPHOMORE YEAR

THE mid-day heat felt good on Rob's back . . . and his sturdy right arm. Warming up, he felt good . . . much like he had felt against Pine Bluff. *Could perfection happen twice in a row?*

Valley Christian's crowd was large as usual . . . and their arrogance was visible as expected. The big crowd knew Valley Christian had just squeaked by Hillsdale in basketball. But they knew they still won every time.

They knew that last year's Sectional baseball game had been surprisingly tough . . . but that was last year . . . Hillsdale was better last year . . . *they lost to Cooley twice, for crying out loud . . . they are seeded #8 . . . to our #1.*

No, they might hang around for a while . . . keep it close . . . but the arrogant crowd felt there was no way Hillsdale would ever beat Valley Christian . . . at anything. Tony Russo knew that, too.

Hillsdale's crowd was hopeful . . . but not convinced they had what it took to topple the Knights. But they hoped . . . and hope was something Hillsdale fans had cultivated for many years . . . hoping to bring "The Pick" back for one . . . but hope had not always, or very often, turned into reality.

So, when Garrett Baker threw the first pitch of the game for a ball to Buck Buckman, the Hillsdale fans saw hope in it . . . hope that today will be the day.

Six pitches later, Baker had retired the Pirates in order, and they were finding their gloves and heading onto the field to play defense.

One pitch later... Rob's perfect game and no-hitter were gone.

Valley Christian's leadoff hitter laced a first-pitch fastball straight back up the middle and into center field for a single. The leadoff hitter... Tony Russo.

Russo stood smirking at Rob from his spot on first base. He turned to Trip, holding him on at first, and sang mockingly, "Turn out the light's the parties over."

Rob looked into Bruce Smithers for the sign. Tony Russo took a huge lead, getting ready to test Bruce's arm down to second.

Rob quickly stepped off the rubber and fired to first.

Tony Russo was caught totally off guard. He tried to get back but, after two steps, looked over to see Trip McHenry, ball in glove, staring at him. Trip reached out and tagged him ... and growled, "This party is just getting started, Russo... grab some pine, meat!"

Russo, totally embarrassed, trotted back to his dugout in shame.

Rob quickly dispatched the next two Valley Christian hitters, and it was scoreless after one. And, after two, and after three, and after the top of four. Hillsdale managed baserunners in every inning, but the first... but were not hitting the ball hard.

In the 3rd, things started to get interesting. Buck Buckman surprised everybody with a one-out bunt down the first baseline. Buck sprinted by the first baseman, who had fielded the ball and glanced at the pitcher. He knew he had him beat to the bag... and now he had to beat the second baseman to the first base.

The second baseman initially got a slow jump. By the time he recovered, Buck had reached first base, and the Pirates had their first hit.

Mark Porter sacrificed Buck to second to bring up Rob Mathews and the first big decision of the game.

It was a quick decision. Walk Mathews intentionally.

Trip McHenry was next, with runners at first and second with two outs.

Garrett Baker had struck Trip on a nasty backdoor slider in the first inning. Trip was called out, having given up on the pitch, thinking it would stay outside.

Having Rob walked intentionally in front of him did not sit well with Trip.

He stepped in, focused, relaxed, and ready . . . and struck out on three pitches . . . the last one being a changeup that dropped off the table as it reached the plate.

The Hillsdale crowd groaned in frustration, and Trip fought the urge to fire his bat straight into the dugout wall.

Valley Christian picked up a leadoff single in the bottom of the 3rd. A sac bunt moved him to second, and a fly ball to Matt Bryant in left was the second out . . . and brought Tony Russo to the plate with a runner in scoring position.

In the stands, Allison Pierce had her first strange feeling about who to root for during a baseball game. *Well, not really,* Allison realized. *I'm definitely rooting for Rob to get Tony out . . . but Tony's such a good friend . . . I like him so much . . . but still . . . I'm rooting for Rob.*

Rob certainly did not share those feelings, and he redoubled his focus and went to work.

A slider at the knees captured a first strike. A changeup dropped low and outside. 1-1 count. A fastball at the letters on the inner half . . . fouled straight back. 1-2 count.

A perfect changeup caught Tony by surprise, and he flailed at it weakly. Strike three.

"Nice swing, Russo," Trip McHenry muttered to Tony as he passed him on the way to the dugout.

In the 4th, Hillsdale threatened again, getting one-out singles by Toby Tyler and Matt Bryant. But Garrett Baker stiffened, struck out Josh Lee, and got Gavin Ford on a sharp comebacker to the mound.

In the bottom of the 4th . . . Hillsdale cracked. Valley Christian's first hitter started the inning with a bloop single to right. Facing the Knight's number three-hitter, Rob got tough and won a grueling ten-pitch battle, finally getting a fly ball to Buck Buckman in short center field.

The next hitter chopped one toward third base, which was played brilliantly by Toby Tyler . . . but his only play was to first for the out. Two outs . . . runner at second.

Next, the number five-hitter. *This is the guy who hit the game-winning homer off me last year,* Rob recalled. *Be careful.*

Rob was careful and induced a little squibber down the third baseline. Rob pounced, trying to get there as soon as possible, but he saw Toby Tyler charging hard from third base. *Toby has the better throw,* Rob thought quickly. *I have to turn and throw. Let him have it.* He got out of Toby's way.

Right decision. Wrong result. Toby's throw to first was wild and skidded past Trip McHenry at first base and down the right field line. By the time Gavin Ford retrieved the ball and got it back to the infield, the baserunner had scored, and the hitter was perched at second base. Valley Christian 1, Hillsdale 0.

Toby Tyler was crushed.

The Hillsdale crowd was crushed.

Valley Christian fans yawned and felt some relief. *That should do it,* they figured.

On to the top of the 5th, and Buck Buckman was at it again, serving a fastball into right for a leadoff hit. Sac bunt by Mark Porter . . . intentional walk to Rob Mathews.

Trip McHenry seething.

A nice and neat 4-6-3 double play. Inning over.

Trip McHenry was ready to explode.

The Hillsdale crowd groaned in frustration. *Not again!!!*

CHAPTER 64
MAY-SOPHOMORE YEAR

*A*N easy bottom of the 5th for Rob, although he hit a batter with two outs. His change squirted away from him, but he recovered nicely and got a swinging third strike on a perfect change to the next hitter to end the inning.

On to the 6th, and Hillsdale squandered a leadoff single by Bruce Smithers . . . the Pirates hitters were never able to advance him past first base.

In the bottom half, Rob retired the first two hitters quickly and then faced the number four-hitter . . . the catcher last year that was so snide . . . so cocky . . . telling Rob that Hillsdale would never beat Valley Christian . . . at anything. *Yeah . . . that guy.*

He took Rob deep. An inside fastball at the belt. Designed to get in on his hands. Bit off too much of the plate and the catcher turned on it and launched it far over the left field fence. 2-0 Valley Christian.

Valley Christian on their feet. Hillsdale not. Heads bowed. Hope fading.

A quick out later . . . Hillsdale in their dugout. Last chance.

Crowd quiet.

Dugout quiet . . . but focused . . . relaxed . . . confident . . .

And angry!

***

*T*HE afternoon breeze was starting to pick up a little, much to the delight of the fans in the bleachers.

"It's getting a little hot out here," one snotty Valley Christian mother said. "Let's finish these guys off so we can go lay out at the pool."

Hearty laughter all around and nods of agreement.

On the other side of the bleachers . . . was despair and depression . . . and maybe a little resignation. "This is Valley Christian, after all," was heard throughout the stands. "They gave it a good fight . . . but they weren't supposed to win."

"We're not done here," Rob Mathews growled in the dugout. "Come on . . . this pitcher's not that good."

"That's right . . . get me an at-bat," Trip McHenry pleaded.

Back in the stands, Emily and Allison sat downcast.

"I didn't really think we would beat Valley Christian today," Emily said dismally. "I don't know, though . . . somehow . . . I thought we might . . . these guys seem to do some amazing things with their backs to the wall!"

"I know," Allison agreed. "We're just so used to Rob coming through in the end . . . "Wonder Boy" . . . you know. Do you think there is any way that can happen today . . . ?"

"Be a pretty big job," Emily said. "Not sure they can against this team . . ."

They nodded in sorrowful agreement.

"RALLY CAP TIME!!!" blared in their ears.

It was, of course, Grandpa Russell.

"LET'S GO! GET THOSE RALLY CAPS ON!!!" Grandpa Russell bellowed for all to hear.

Far fewer Hillsdale fans than normal heeded his call. Even Emily and Allison had to be shamed into it with a fierce stare from Grandpa Russell.

The Valley Christian fans pointed and laughed.

Valley Christian took the field, and Garrett Baker confidently climbed on top of the mound . . . ready to put Hillsdale out of their misery.

Gavin Ford led off. Pop-out to second base.

Huge groan from the Hillsdale side of the bleachers.

Buck Buckman was next, and the Hillsdale fans showed some spark. Lazy fly ball to left field. Two outs.

Another groan . . . many people starting to collect their things and head home.

Mark Porter up. Last chance. Strike one. Strike two. Hillsdale down to their last strike.

Turn out the light's . . . the party's over . . .

CHAPTER 65

MAY-SOPHOMORE YEAR

"**C'MON**, Mark!" Rob Mathews shouted. "Stay ready . . . hit it hard."

Garrett Baker wound up and fired . . . smash . . . to first . . . over his head and into the right field corner!!! Porter dashed toward first, saw he had at least a double, and flew around the bag. Coming into second, he looked at Coach Wilson at third and saw him putting up the stop sign.

Mark stopped on the bag and looked into the dugout, punching his fist in the air.

"WE HAVE LIFE!!!" Grandpa Russell screamed.

"Rob will do it," Allison said but stopped short. She looked up and saw the four-finger sign . . . they were walking him intentionally . . . again.

Rob saw the signal and fought not to scream. *NO!!! You're not supposed to walk the tying run . . . that's not good baseball!*

"Grandpa Russell, why are they walking, Rob," Allison asked in confusion. "Isn't that against the "baseball rules" you talked about?"

"Yes, it is, Allison," Grandpa Russell answered, clearly frustrated Rob was not going to be given a chance to hit . . . again. "The coach is playing the percentages . . . playing a hunch. He thinks his pitcher will have an easier time getting Trip out than Rob . . . and so far, that's been the case."

Allison nodded in understanding . . . but now focused her concern on Trip. *He's had a bad day,* Allison thought. *This could make it a terrible day.*

"Time out!" Coach Wilson blared, motioning Mark Porter and Rob Mathews to join him and Trip McHenry in foul territory halfway to third base.

Coach Wilson, excited but calm, looked at the trio.

"You guys," Coach Wilson said, motioning to Mark and Rob, "are off on contact. Mark, you be careful. If Trip hits it too hard, I may have to hold you up at third . . . you're an important run . . . but you don't mean much if Rob can't score."

The pair nodded.

"Rob . . . if Trip's hit is a gapper or something down a line . . . I'm going to be aggressive with you . . . we have to take our chance here to get a tie. Be ready to fly."

Rob nodded.

"Trip . . . when you hit it . . . make sure you motor immediately . . . but once you get to second . . . be a little cautious . . . if these two have scored . . . we'll be tied, and you'll be in scoring position for Bruce."

"Got it?" Coach Wilson asked all three. They nodded, and as Rob and Mark retreated toward first and second, Coach Wilson tugged at Trip's sleeve, keeping him close.

"Trip," Coach Wilson said, leaning in close to whisper loudly so that Trip could hear him over the crowd's roar.

"We need a three-pointer to win at the buzzer," Coach Wilson said, smiling broadly. "Think you're up for it?"

Trip's head snapped up at the basketball allusion.

"I think you are," Coach Wilson continued. "Focus. Relax. Remember what you and Rob have worked on in the cage all year."

Trip nodded.

"You are the man, Trip," Coach added. "That's why we call you Trip! Go do it!"

Feeling more confident, Trip grinned and turned back to the plate.

"Hey, McHenry," came a low shout from Tony Russo, standing alone near the pitcher's mound. "Don't think too much about your little promise to never lose to us . . . choker . . . you guys cannot beat us. What'll it be this time, loser, strike out or double play . . . oh, that's right . . . you already have two outs . . . strike out, it is!"

Trip tuned him out and headed to the plate. Looked down at Coach Wilson and saw him smiling back at him, urging him to do well.

Trip settled in the box . . . stared out at Garrett Baker.

Strike one. Change up. Trip way out in front. Loud cackle from Tony Russo at short. Hillsdale crowd groans. Valley Christian crowd slightly bored.

Called strike two. Fastball at the knees. Outside corner. Hillsdale crowd moans. Valley Christian fans are still slightly bored . . . but they rise as one for the final strike . . . the final out . . . and they can move onto the Semifinals next week.

"PING!!!!"

Trip McHenry crushed a changeup clearly over the second baseman's glove and headed for the right-center field gap. Mark Porter and Rob Mathews are flying around the bases.

Will it make it to the wall? Rob wondered as he rounded second and turned his back on the ball, picking up Coach Wilson in the third base coach's box.

He heard the crowd screaming and saw Mark Porter heading for the plate. Coach Wilson has his arm wind-milling frantically, telling Rob to head for the plate.

Rob rounded third at full speed and, out of the corner of his eye, saw the ball reaching the cutoff man in short right field. *It's the second baseman,* Rob realized in a flash, *weaker arm. Still gotta' hurry. Gonna' be a play at the plate!*

Coach Wilson is dancing down the line with him. Mark Porter is waiting to the side of the plate . . . hoping to coach Rob on whether or not to slide.

The second baseman throws . . . on a line . . . perfect strike . . . going to be close.

Mark Porter waves his arms to the outside part of the plate and yells, "SLIDE!!!"

Rob veers to the back side of the plate and goes into a fadeaway foot-first slide. The catcher grabs the ball just in front of the plate and swipes his glove toward Rob. The umpire slides into position. Looking for contact of glove to runner. None. Looking for contact of runner to plate. Yes . . . just on the edge . . .

"SAFE!!!! SAFE!!!! SAFE!!!!" screams the umpire.

Rob and Mark embrace. Tie score.

Trip McHenry racing from second to third. Trying to beat Tony Russo to the bag. The catcher spots Trip . . . spots Tony Russo . . . rifles a throw to third . . . Tony's there . . . raises his glove to catch . . . swipe tag . . . the ball slides out of his glove.

Trip on his feet . . . heading for the plate . . . Tony Russo scrambles after it . . . turns and throws toward home . . . Trip chugging down the line . . . starts his slide . . . the ball sails over everybody . . . Trip's safe . . . two errors on Russo . . . Hillsdale 3, Valley Christian 2.

Bedlam reigned. Hillsdale fans awoke from their slumber and were delirious with joy. Dancing, laughing, hugging, and screaming at the top of their lungs.

Valley Christian sat in stunned silence . . . suddenly their arrogance was gone . . . they were not supposed to sweat this one. *We'll pull it out,* they thought. But there was doubt seeping in all through the Valley Christian bleachers.

The big catcher looked at Tony Russo in disbelief . . . Tony looked at the ground . . . Garrett Baker stared daggers at Tony Russo . . . and Tony wanted to disappear.

Coach Wilson knew the game was far from over. But he also knew one more thing.

Now . . . it was Hulk Thomas time!

CHAPTER 66
MAY-SOPHOMORE YEAR

*V**ALLEY* Christian was at the lower part of their batting order, with the 6-7-8 hitters coming up first. But . . . as Rob remembered all too well . . . Valley Christian's offense was deep and deadly, one through nine.

Many of them also knew "Tubby" Thomas, and the heckling from the Valley Christian players and fans started as soon as Hulk Thomas walked in from the bullpen.

Calls of "Tubby" rang out for all to hear, and Rob cringed at the name. When Hulk reached the mound, Rob met him and said, "Don't let that bug you, Hulk."

"What?" Hulk answered, his face a mask.

Rob smiled, nodded, and moved out to his shortstop position. Josh Lee, who played short when Rob pitched, slid over to third base, and Toby Tyler moved to the bench.

No one was more relieved than Toby to be pulled from third base. The slick-fielding catcher was out of position there . . . and knew it. Next year, with Bruce Smithers gone, he planned to claim the catcher's spot and never have to play third again!

As Hulk Thomas completed his final warmups, the crowd noise started to ramp up. On the Hillsdale side, a loud excited buzz . . . with an undercurrent of worry . . . rose from the fans, most of whom were already standing.

"Do you have a Non-Rally Cap idea for our defense?" Allison asked Grandpa Russell, only half-kidding.

"Oh, now that would just be silly," Grandpa Russell teased back, amid nervous laughter from those around her who heard the exchange

The Valley Christian side erupted when their first hitter approached the plate, and they rose to their feet in anticipation of a game-winning rally to end this craziness. But there was doubt on that side of the bleachers.

Both sides of the bleachers were on their feet when Hulk Thomas threw a nasty cutter right past the Knight's number six-hitter. Some on Valley Christian's side sat down . . . and more joined them when Hulk fired another strike . . . this one called, right past the hitter.

But those who had sat down leaped to their feet in excitement when Hulk's third pitch was blooped over Trip McHenry's head at first and fell in front of an onrushing Gavin Ford in right for a leadoff single.

Now, some on the Hillsdale side sat down . . . and started fretting about what would happen next.

The Hillsdale side groaned as the number seven-hitter hit Hulk's first pitch back up the middle and on the way to center field.

Out of nowhere, there was Rob Mathews, stretching as far as he could to glove the ball, turn 360 degrees, and fire a strike to first, where a stretching Trip McHenry nipped the hitter for out number one. But . . . Valley Christian had the tying run at second base.

The number eight-hitter was scrappy . . . and he made Hulk work, fouling off several pitches . . . and then slapped a soft liner into center.

Valley Christian's runner at second had to hesitate. Buck was playing shallow center field. Finally, he saw the ball was going to fall, and he tore for third . . . making a huge turn around third base . . . but he scrambled back when Buck sent a perfect throw toward home. Trip McHenry cut the throw, enabling Hillsdale to keep the winning run at first.

The Hillsdale crowd sighed heavily, most of them sitting down . . . some with their faces in their hands . . . others afraid to look.

Rob called time and went to the mound. Coach Wilson trotted out to join them . . . and the rest of the infield circled Hulk on the mound.

"They haven't hit the ball hard yet, Hulk," Rob said immediately. "Keep doing what you're doing . . . we'll get em'!"

"He's right, Hulk," said a surprisingly cool and calm Coach Wilson. "Your stuff looks good . . . keep it up!"

Hulk nodded with determination.

"Infield in, guys," Coach Wilson said. "You guys know the drill . . . Trip, hold that runner close at first!"

They all nodded in understanding.

"This is it, guys . . . get an out . . . stop that runner at third from scoring," Coach Wilson added. "Get er' done!"

The meeting broke up, and the infield returned to their spots.

Rob looked in at the hitter . . . the number nine-hitter . . . and the memories flooded back from last year's Sectional loss to Valley Christian. *Number nine-hitter . . . home run . . . game and season over. Not again!*

CHAPTER 67
MAY-SOPHOMORE YEAR

HULK Thomas stood stoically on the mound, hearing the taunts of the Valley Christian players and fans, and it made him grit his teeth. *Not this time,* he thought. *Not this time.*

He stepped on top of the hill and peered in for the sign. Bruce Smithers flashed a cutter on the outside corner. Hulk nodded yes and threw.

The pitch was perfect . . . nipping the outside corner on the black with movement running outside. Valley Christian's hitter took the bait and lunged at the pitch . . . and flared it toward the right field line.

Trip McHenry, crouched by first, came off the bag with the pitch . . . saw the hit heading over his head . . . reversed course and leaped as high as he possibly could.

The crowd gasped . . . those sitting rose as one . . . Trip stretched . . . ball hit leather . . . Trip came down . . . ball in glove and dove toward the first base bag in hopes of a double play.

"SAFE!" the first base umpire screamed.

"LOOK HOME!!!!" Trip heard through a haze. His eyes darted toward the plate, and he saw the runner at third, making like he might head home. Trip bounced up and ran the ball toward third, and the runner scampered back to the bag.

Two outs. First and third. Tony Russo advancing to the plate. Tony Russo smiled out at the mound. He mouthed the words, "Times up, Tubby. You will never get me out."

Hulk Thomas smiled at him . . . Tony Russo looked out at him in amazement.

"Bring it," Tony said.

The vast crowd was momentarily spent. Both sides knew how close that play was to tying the game at three or ending it with a double play for a Hillsdale win. Now, they all took a deep breath. Exhaled. Started to buzz. Started to scream. Started to pray. No one sat down.

Hulk Thomas looked around at his infield . . . now back at regular depth. He looked at Rob . . . who looked back and nodded.

"You got this guy," Rob yelled. "Use everything!"

Hulk nodded back at Rob.

Hulk stood tall on the mound and looked in for a sign . . . and threw a perfect changeup to Tony Russo . . . whose eyes bugged out at the sight of the pitch.

Called strike one.

Cutter. Outside corner at the knees. Called strike two.

Tony Russo shook his head. *This is not the Tubby I remember,* Tony thought. *Choke up. Short swing. Put it in play.*

Four-seam fastball . . . up and in. Ball one.

Cutter. Down and in. Just missed. Ball two.

Cutter. Letter high. Outside part of the plate . . . maybe not a strike. Fouled off. 2-2 count.

Backdoor cutter. Starting outside . . . moving back toward the plate. Knee-high. Perfect pitch. Just off the black. Ball three.

I've got him now, Tony Russo thought. *He can't nibble . . . he can't walk me . . . moves the tying run into scoring position. No more back door stuff . . . especially no more changeups.*

"Bring it, Tubby," Tony shouts out to the mound. "Bring it!"

The crowd, at this point, was at a fever pitch. Hillsdale's fans were pleading for Hulk Thomas and the defense to get this one final out. This would be the first time Hillsdale had beaten Valley Christian . . . at anything.

This can't be happening, thought many a Valley Christian fan. *Tony will come through. He always does . . . especially against Tubby Thomas.*

Hulk rubbed up the ball. Peered in for the sign. The crowd ramped up into one colossal roar.

Cutter. Inside on the hands. Fouled back.

The crowd takes a breath. Allison and Emily look at each other . . . both with a painful half-smile, half-grimace on their faces. *You call this fun,* Allison suddenly thinks. *This is torture.*

Cutter. Outside corner. On the knees. Perfect pitch. Fouled off.

This time the crowd doesn't breathe. The roar is enormous.

Cutter. Outside corner. On the knees. Perfect pitch. Fouled off.

The crowd is exhausted . . . but they keep ramping up for each new pitch.

Cutter. Inside. Moving back toward the black. Emergency swing. Topped foul down the third baseline.

Cutter. Outside corner at knees. Barely got a piece.

Changeup. Outside corner at the knees . . .

CHAPTER 68
MAY-SOPHOMORE YEAR

***S*TRIKE** three!!!!

Called.

Tony Russo in shock.

The entire crowd gasped. Then a long pause while what just happened sunk in.

Bedlam.

Euphoria in Hillsdale.

Stunned silence.

Disbelief for Valley Christian.

Trip McHenry, standing with his arms straight up to the sky, screaming for joy.

Rob Mathews, pumping his fist and heading for the mound.

Hulk Thomas staring at Tony Russo . . . smiling at Tony's distraught look. Tony banging down his bat and helmet and stomping away.

Valley Christian fans, all sitting with their mouths hanging open . . . watching the Hillsdale fans streaming happily onto the field . . . their field . . . to celebrate a win . . . over Valley Christian.

Unreal.

The Pirates in a pile behind the pitcher's mound . . . Hulk Thomas at the bottom.

Coach Dave Wilson . . . hiding a few tears . . . standing back and letting the experience flow over him . . . enjoying watching his kids celebrate.

The crowd reaches the field . . . reaches the team.

Hugging. Back slapping. Dancing. Shrieking with delight.

Lisa Cruz reaches Rob first. Big hug. Big smile.

Donnie Fields and Christina Craft are next.

Allison is next. Huge hug. Electric charge. Big smile. Rob melts. Gets carried apart from Allison by the crowd. Runs into Trip. Trip turns around. Bear hug.

"You see . . . I told you we'd never lose to Valley Christian again!" Trip shouts.

Rob grins back.

"Yeah, but you still need to keep your big mouth shut," Rob yells back in laughter.

Trip gives Rob a big thumbs-up and then gets carried away by the crowd.

***

BY Sunday, Hillsdale was starting to settle down. The little town had partied hearty on Saturday afternoon, into the evening, and for some past midnight.

Sunday morning, as usual, Rob's Grandparents, Mom, and Trip McHenry sat around the breakfast table, reliving yesterday's glory.

Grandpa Russell was glowing with pride for both of his "boys" and spent much of the morning telling them how proud he was of them.

The only negative came at the end of Dan Mercer's column in Sunday's *Hillsdale Express*.

"As huge as this win was today . . . and don't get me wrong here . . . beating Valley Christian is maybe the best thing that has ever happened to Hillsdale baseball . . . we still have to win two more games to get that elusive first Sectional Championship. And don't look past #5 Kingwood, our next opponent, on Wednesday. They started slowly and nursed along a pitcher . . . much like Dave Wilson's great work with Hulk Thomas. But Kingwood's pitcher, Chad Moranda, is a starter and has been near unhittable since the middle of the season. They have shutout both their opponents in the Sectionals . . . including a very impressive two-hitter against the #4 seed, Freeman, who arguably, has one of the best offenses in the Section. Beating Valley Christian was great . . . but we haven't accomplished anything yet!"

"I don't like hearing it, guys . . . but he's right . . . Kingwood will be tough!" Grandpa Russell said gravely.

Rob and Trip knew he was right . . . but that wasn't until Wednesday, and they had a fun day of whiffle ball and watching the Giants-Dodgers game in mind with a bunch of guys, and they had hurried off early.

***

*S***UNDAY** evening was "Movie Night" at Rob's, and his Mom made a great dinner. Rob chose *Major League* . . . a movie the guys loved but left Emily, Linda, and Allison less pleased.

As the movie ended, it was clear everyone was exhausted from a packed last week or so. Trip hustled out the door to get in some last-minute studying for finals . . . and Rob and Allison were headed in that direction as well.

"Well," Allison said as she and Rob helped clean up after the movie. "This is our last "Movie Night" for a while . . . can you spend the summer coming up with a better movie than tonight?"

Allison said it with a twinkle in her eye, and Rob caught the look and laughed.

"I'll try," Rob replied. "It is weird to think we won't be seeing each other for almost three months,"

"I know," Allison answered. *At least he knows how long it will be,* Allison thought. *He must be thinking about it!*

"You sure you won't be here next Sunday?" Rob asked. "Maybe get one more of "Allison's Classic Movies" in before you go."

They both laughed.

"No, I don't think so. It looks like it will be Friday . . . but no later than Saturday," Allison said.

Rob nodded, understanding for the first time that Allison was going to be gone . . . for three months. *If I'm going to talk to her about how I feel . . . I better do it soon. Maybe, now? Tomorrow? No, after Sectionals . . . or at least after Wednesday's game.*

"You'll just have to do "Movie Night" without me," Allison said, eyes twinkling again. "Maybe you and Trip can get your bad movies out of the way this summer."

Rob laughed and realized he hadn't been listening. *I'm going to miss her . . . a lot.*

"Allison . . . let's go!" Linda Pierce called out from the kitchen.

Allison got up to leave, and both stood awkwardly, not knowing what to do.

Should I hug him? Allison wondered. *We've been doing that more . . . the one at the game was great!*

Should I hug her? Rob wondered. *I want to . . . but I don't want it to be weird.*

"Allison! Let's go," Linda interrupted them. "You've got homework to get to . . . and so does Rob. Let's get going."

"OK, OK, Mom, I'm coming . . ." Allison said feebly.

"Good night, Rob . . . I'll see you in the morning," Allison sighed.

"Good night, Allison!" Rob answered with a crooked smile.

She gave him her best smile and waved as she walked out with her Mom.

Something has changed with Allison . . . I don't know what it is . . . she looks the same . . . but different somehow. I kinda' like it . . . I kinda' like her, Rob thought.

"Whatcha' thinkin' about big fella," Emily said, snapping him out of his thoughts.

"Oh, um . . . nothing," Rob replied.

"Come on," Emily chided. "You're thinking about Allison, right?"

"Well, yeah," Rob admitted.

"Did you tell her yet?" Emily asked.

"Nah," Rob replied. "I want to wait until after Sectionals."

"You might run out of time . . . you know they leave Friday or Saturday . . . the finals are Saturday."

"If we can get by Kingwood," Rob pointed out. "But you're right . . . I'll talk to her Thursday after practice . . . once we get by Kingwood."

"Sounds like a plan," Emily said with a smile. "Now, go hit the books . . . you've got a final tomorrow!"

CHAPTER 69
MAY-SOPHOMORE YEAR

*B**UT* Hillsdale was not able to get by Kingwood.

The Pirates ran into a buzz saw on Wednesday afternoon at the Hillsdale Baseball/Softball complex . . . and it wasn't pretty.

The visiting team on their own home field . . . by virtue of being the lower seed . . . was weird. But while Kingwood's pitcher Chad Moranda was on fire . . . Jose Rivera was not. And that was weird, too.

Moranda started the game in style with a strikeout of Buck Buckman . . . only the fourth strikeout of the season for Buck . . . and it didn't vastly improve after that. Mark Porter popped up, and Rob Mathews lined out . . . and then it went downhill.

Jose Rivera did not have his good stuff . . . and by the time Coach Wilson had figured that out, it was 4-0 Kingwood.

When Hillsdale had finally collected their first hit and baserunner, a solid single to center by Rob Mathews in the 4th inning, it was 7-0, and the huge Hillsdale crowd had realized Hillsdale's run at the Sectional title was probably over.

Three non-productive innings later, it was official . . . and Kingwood walked away with a 7-0 victory and a trip to the Sectional Finals.

Hillsdale got to pack up their gear and turn in their uniforms.

***

THE Hillsdale crowd, though, is nothing if not faithful. About 90% stayed in their seats while Coach Wilson gave his last postgame speech of the year.

Sensing the crowd was still in place, Coach Wilson gathered his team and had them emerge as one and turn and face the throng still in the bleachers . . . and the fans erupted with a roar that would have made folks downtown think the Pirates had just completed a win.

The crowd kept the applause up for a solid 90 seconds, and many on the team . . . and many in the crowd were fighting back tears.

Finally, the roar subsided, and fans started trickling down onto the field to see their sons, boyfriends, and friends and congratulate them on a great season.

It was not the celebration the Hillsdale fans envisioned, but it was touching and meaningful just the same.

In the big crowd, Rob got hugs and handshakes from lots of folks and friends . . . and from his Grandma and Grandpa Russell . . . who were better able to maneuver through the crowd in this scenario as opposed to the madhouses of the Pine Bluff and Valley Christian celebrations.

He gazed over and saw his Mom near the dugout, talking with Coach Wilson, and he smiled. *I wonder if she's ready yet? I hope so,* Rob thought.

Around 20 minutes later, the crowd had thinned, and Rob sat staring out onto the field from his favorite perch on the dugout bench.

It's been quite a year, he thought, reflecting on the long school year and the three grueling sports seasons . . . *successful seasons, yes . . . but certainly with some ups and downs. I sure wish we hadn't missed all those opportunities this baseball season. Missed chances all year long!*

Trip McHenry stuck his head into the dugout.

"Hey, guys are heading down to Pop's . . . you coming?" Trip asked.

"Yeah," Rob answered with a smile. "I'll meet you down there . . . save me a spot."

Trip gave him a thumbs up.

This time last year, Rob recalled, *that guy was just a figment of our imaginations . . . now look at him. I'm so glad he's here.*

"Rob?"

Rob snapped his head up . . . it was Allison. *Maybe now is the time to tell her . . .*

"You OK, Rob?" Allison asked as she tiptoed toward him.

"Yeah," Rob answered, suddenly a little weary. "Much better to lose like this . . . than the way Valley Christian did last week . . . or Pine Bluff did a couple of weeks ago."

"I guess that's true . . . still, I'm sorry you lost today," Allison said sincerely.

"I know. Thanks, Allison. I'll be fine," Rob said.

"At least this way, I know I won't miss the Sectional Championship game on Saturday," Allison said.

"Yeah . . . always a silver lining, right," Rob replied.

"You sure you are OK?" Allison asked with real concern. "If you need a friend . . . you know . . . I can stay . . . but . . ."

"But?" Rob prompted.

"I've got to go study . . . I'm taking my last final tonight . . . just in case . . . you know . . . the trip to Europe," Allison said quickly.

"I thought you were leaving Friday or Saturday?" Rob asked, suddenly concerned.

"Yeah, we are," Allison said with a smile. "But my dad said I needed to get this done tonight, just in case."

"Oh, OK," Rob said, noticing Allison needed to go.

"Hey, maybe we can get together tomorrow after school," Rob said softly. "Kind of a going away get-together." *That will be perfect,* Rob thought. *I can talk to her about us then.*

"I'd really like that, Rob," Allison said, misting up. *That will be perfect.*

"Thanks, Ally . . . thanks for always being here," Rob said.

"My pleasure," Allison spouted, teasing him a little. "I've got to run . . . see you tomorrow . . . we can walk to school in the morning!"

"Great . . . bye, Ally," Rob said as she bounded up the dugout stairs and disappeared.

Ally . . . Ally . . . I love it when he calls me that, Allison thought all the way home.

CHAPTER 70
MAY-SOPHOMORE YEAR

"So, did you talk to Allison?" Emily quizzed Rob after he got home from Pop's.

"No," Rob said. "She was in a rush to study . . . she is taking her last final tonight. We're going to hang out tomorrow after school . . . maybe go for a walk or something . . . I'll talk to her about it then."

"Your mind is made up?" Emily asked. "You sure you want a girlfriend? You sure you want it to be Allison?"

"Mom . . . you love, Allison!?" Rob exclaimed.

"Yes, I do . . . I just want you to be sure," Emily explained.

"I am," Rob replied. "Ever since she said told me she'd never date me if she was hot . . . because the way a girl looked was all I cared about . . . well, I realized being hot shouldn't matter either way . . . you either like someone or you don't. I really like Allison, Mom . . . I mean really . . . and I want to let her know how much I like her even though she's not hot!"

"Whoa, be careful there, Rob," Emily said. "Allison might not take it too well to be told she's not hot . . ."

Rob laughed.

"I won't say it that way, Mom," Rob said. "Allison . . . she'll know . . . I won't have to say it . . . but if I ask her out . . . well, she'll know I like her for her . . . not how she looks. I want her to know how much I like her . . . how good she makes me feel . . . how much I want to make her happy. I think she'll like that . . . I think it will make her happy."

"That sounds better," Emily said with relief. "The other thing I worry about is . . . are you doing this because you feel sorry for her? I don't want you to do something nice . . . only to crush her in a week if you lose interest . . . or change your mind."

"No, I don't feel sorry for her, Mom," Rob answered. "I just think she's great! I can't stop thinking about her. And, if I can make her happy . . . well, that's even better."

Emily laughed and nodded and pulled Rob in for a hug.

"You're going to be a great husband someday," Emily said as she squeezed him tight.

***

THE next morning, Rob was awakened very early, sensing movement on his bed.

It was his Mom, and she was gently shaking him.

"Mom . . . what . . . did I forget my alarm?" Rob mumbled through his sleepiness.

"No, no," Emily said softly. "I've got some bad news and wanted you to have time to process it before you go to school."

Rob was instantly awake and worried.

"What happened . . . are Grandpa and Grandma OK?" Rob asked with trepidation.

"Yes, yes, they're fine," Emily soothed.

"What then?" Rob asked anxiously.

"Allison's gone . . ." Emily told him quietly.

"Gone...missing...what do you mean gone?" Rob asked, starting to feel panic brewing.

"No, no," Emily laughed. "You are quite the Doomsday Man, aren't you?"

"What do you mean, gone?" Rob asked, calming down.

"She left with her family for Europe this morning," Emily announced.

"What?" Rob asked. "She wasn't supposed to leave until Friday or Saturday . . . I was going to . . . we were going to talk this afternoon . . . she can't be gone."

"Afraid she is, big guy," Emily said. "They should be getting on their first flight pretty soon . . . then a layover in Chicago for a couple hours and then off to Europe."

"Well, maybe I could call her now," Rob said, scrambling for his phone.

"Wait a minute, Buster," Emily said, bringing him back to the bed. "This is not something you tell a girl . . . especially a girl like Allison . . . over the phone, or in a text . . . or an email. This is something you do in person."

"But," Rob protested. "She won't be back for three months! I can't wait that long!"

"You're not going to see her anyway, honey," Emily explained. "It wouldn't be right to tell Allison now . . . and then be apart for three months. Besides, Allison is going to want to see your face when you tell her . . . you're going to want to see her face . . . how it will light up . . . you need to do this in person, honey."

"I missed my chance," Rob said, welling up. "What if . . . I don't get another chance?"

"You will, Rob," Emily said sincerely. "Something tells me with Allison . . . she'll welcome this news whenever you get the chance . . . now . . . or at the end of August when she gets home . . . but . . . you owe it to her . . . to tell in person."

Emily watched as Rob took it all in and finally nodded in agreement.

"OK," Rob said with resignation. "I get it . . . I need to do it in person . . . I just can't believe I missed my chance to tell her now."

"It will all work out fine in time," Emily said, stroking his hair and hugging him.

***

ROB looked at the clock and saw he had an hour, so he took his time getting ready for school . . . thought about Allison . . . took a quick look at his notes for today's final, and went downstairs to grab some breakfast.

He walked into the kitchen and saw his Mom standing at the kitchen sink, staring off into space . . . looking like she was going to a party.

Her hair was combed perfectly, and her makeup was on . . . something he didn't usually see before he left for school. She was wearing a summer dress, and he could smell a hint of her perfume. *She looks beautiful,* Rob thought. *Where is she going?*

"Oh, Rob, hi," Emily mumbled distractedly. "Hey, do I remember correctly that Coach Wilson has a couple of open periods in the morning?" Emily asked out of the blue.

"Yeah," Rob drawled out slowly. "I . . . think his first class is at . . . let's see . . . 3rd period . . . so 9:50 am. Why?"

"Oh, I just need to run something by him," Emily said, slightly embarrassed. "I'm going to just run over there now,"

"Uh, OK," Rob said, clearly puzzled, as he watched her head out the door . . . just as Trip bounded in.

Emily said hello, but moved quickly past him and down the sidewalk, walking briskly.

"Wow! She looks hot!" Trip said in appreciation.

"Trip! That's my Mom," Rob retorted.

"I know, I know!" Trip laughed. "Just sayin' . . . she's hot."

Rob punched him in the arm playfully, and they headed out the door to school.

CHAPTER 71
MAY-SOPHOMORE YEAR

***E*MILY** Mathews walked quickly toward school and thought, *Am I sure I want to do this? Yes, yes, I'm sure. It's been long enough . . . almost two years since Jack died. After seeing Rob this morning . . . it's time. I don't want to miss out on my chance.*

She made her way to Dave Wilson's office at the end of the corridor next to the gym. *What if he's not here? I can catch him later. What if he says no? Don't think about that.*

Emily reached Dave's door . . . hesitated . . . and rapped softly.

"Come in," came the response from inside the office.

Emily slowly inched the door open . . . *should I run now before he sees me? No!* She pushed it open, and Dave Wilson looked up in startled surprise.

"Emily," Dave said, jumping up quickly with concern on his face. "Is everything OK?"

"Yes, yes," Emily said, smiling shyly. "Everything's fine. Do you have a minute? This will just take a minute."

"Sure, what can I do for you," Dave replied, noticing that Emily looked stunning this morning. *My gosh, she's gorgeous,* he thought as he wondered what was up.

"Well, uh, Dave," Emily started, clearly uneasy. Finally, she braced herself, smiled broadly at Dave, and continued. "You know how I told you I would let you know . . . when I was ready to start, uh . . . dating?"

"Uh, yeah," Dave said with a smile. "You said you'd phone to let me know."

"I know . . . I know," Emily laughed. "But I thought it was better to do it in person."

"So . . ." Dave prompted, laughing softly.

"So, I wanted to let you . . . you know . . . I'm ready to start dating," Emily said bashfully, raising her eyes and smiling at him. "If you'd like to . . . maybe you could give me a call sometime, and we could get together."

Dave paused and smiled at Emily.

"I will do that," Dave said, staring into her eyes. "Yes, I will definitely do that."

"OK, uh, thanks," Emily said, feeling embarrassed and ready for this part to be over. "I'll wait for your call . . . thanks!"

They lingered . . . staring at each other for a few moments until Emily abruptly turned and walked through the door and started walking down the corridor to get some much-needed fresh air.

I need to get out of here before I run into Rob and Trip. Emily thought in panic. *I don't want to see them now. What was I thinking doing this at school?*

As she walked, she heard her phone ring . . . ring again . . .

"Hey, Emily," she heard Dave Wilson call out behind her. "Aren't you going to answer your phone?"

Flustered, Emily reached into her purse, fumbled until she found her phone, and stared at the screen.

The Caller ID read: **Coach Wilson**.

Turning around, she answered her phone and lifted it to her ear. She saw Dave Wilson, framed in his door, grinning at her . . . with his phone in his hand, his hand to his ear.

"Hello," she said into her phone as she walked slowly toward Dave.

"Hi, Emily?" Coach Wilson asked playfully.

"Yes," Emily replied coyly.

"This is Dave Wilson," Dave grinned.

"Hi, Dave, what a surprise!" Emily laughed.

They both smiled at each other.

"What can I do for you, Dave?" Emily asked with a small smile.

"Well, Emily, I was wondering . . . wondering if you'd like to have dinner with me tonight?" Coach Wilson asked confidently.

"Tonight . . . oh, gosh, Dave . . . I'm sorry, Dave . . . I have plans tonight," Emily said slyly.

Dave's smile disappeared in confusion.

Emily paused, letting the statement sink in . . . then smiled coyly.

"But I'm free for breakfast!" Emily exclaimed.

Dave Wilson quickly recovered from his shock.

"Breakfast sounds great," Dave said as he quickly closed the door to his office.

Emily turned and started strolling down the corridor. She punched "end call" on her phone and said over her shoulder, "Thanks for calling, Dave."

Dave hurried to catch up . . . and opened the door for Emily, and they stepped out into the morning sunshine.

END OF BOOK SIX

About Author

A sports fanatic since early childhood, Mac grew up watching the great San Francisco Giants teams of Willie Mays, among others. Also on the watchlist; the San Francisco (now Golden State) Warriors, the San Francisco 49ers, and Oakland Raiders. A decent athlete, he played basketball for Pacific Grove High and spent 10 years playing men's open-division fastpitch softball. In his 30s, he began his coaching career, which spanned over 40 teams with kids as young as six all the way up through high school girls softball at Carmel High, where he headed the program from 1997-2006. After retiring from active coaching, Mac spent several years giving coaching clinics on topics including fundamentals, philosophy, practice organization, and team building for high school and youth league coaches. The insights into high school kids and coaching proved invaluable for these books. Add to that six children and 13 grandchildren, and he definitely knows kids!

Mac's writing "career" began in high school as the editor of his school newspaper during his senior year. The idea of writing a series like this stemmed from reading the classic Chip Hilton books written by Clair Bee, mostly in the 1950s. From start to finish, the 12-book Rob Mathews Sports Series project "only" took 28 years to complete . . . family, coaching, and work kept getting in the way!

A native of California's Bay Area and Central Coast, Mac and his wife Suzanne (Suzy) have a home in the Sierra Nevada Foothills east of Sacramento, the setting for the series. Ironically, this area was chosen as a setting for the series 25 years before acquiring the home.

Also By

The Rob Mathews Sports Series

FRESHMAN YEAR

1. FRESH START 2. GAME PLAN 3. TEAM PLAYERS

SOPHOMORE YEAR

4. LAST CHANCE 5. TRIP ARRIVES 6. MISSED CHANCES

JUNIOR YEAR

7. ALMOST PERFECT 8. NEW NORMAL 9. BEST CASE

SENIOR YEAR

10. SUDDEN DEATH 11. FINALLY RIGHT 12. DECISION TIME

ALL BOOKS AVAILABLE IN E-BOOK, PAPERBACK & HARDBACK FORMATS

REVIEWS WELCOMED AND APPRECIATED ON BOOKSELLER WEBSITE

Made in United States
Troutdale, OR
11/24/2024